In this fascinating study, Edwards ventures far and wide, drawing on a sophisticated array of social and cultural theorists to critically dissect the PR profession. She thus pushes PR scholarship far beyond its comfort zone and into exciting and challenging new directions.

Aeron Davis, *Professor, Goldsmiths University of London, UK*

Lee Edwards makes a mark as a major sociologist of public relations with this stimulating and challenging book on diversity (or the lack of it) in the profession. Skilfully integrating theory and practice, she offers an incisive analysis of race, racism, and identity politics in a field where such issues are usually hidden away in the margins.

Debashish Munshi, *Professor, The University of Waikato, New Zealand*

Dr Edwards' book makes a series of important contributions and provides a cultural and institutional history of the development of public relations as an emblematic profession for our times. It engages in a sophisticated and personal way with leading gender, critical race and diversity theories, locating these debates in the contemporary reorganization of professional occupations, and of the political economy more broadly. And all of this is delivered through a clear and very compelling narrative.

Daniel Muzio, *Professor, Newcastle University, UK*

Power, Diversity and Public Relations

Power, Diversity and Public Relations addresses the lack of diversity in PR by revealing the ways in which power operates within the occupation to construct archetypal practitioner identities, occupational belonging and exclusion. It explores the ways in which the field is normatively constructed through discourse, and examines how the experiences of practitioners whose ethnicity and class differ from the 'typical' PR background shape alternative understandings of the occupation and their place within it.

The book applies theoretical perspectives, ranging from Bourdieuvian and occupational sociology to postcolonial and critical race theory, to a variety of empirical data from the UK PR industry. Diversity emerges as a product of the dialectics between occupational structures, norms and practitioners' reactions to those constraints; it follows that improving diversity is best understood as an exercise in democracy, where all practitioner voices are heard, valued and encompass the potential for change.

This insightful text will be essential reading for researchers and students in Public Relations, Communications, Media Studies, and Promotional Industries, as well as all scholars interested in the sociology of race and work relations.

Lee Edwards is Associate Professor at the School of Media and Communication, University of Leeds, UK.

Routledge New Directions in Public Relations and Communication Research
Edited by Kevin Moloney

Routledge New Directions in Public Relations and Communication Research is a new forum for the publication of books of original research in PR and related types of communication. Its remit is to publish critical and challenging responses to continuities and fractures in contemporary PR thinking and practice, and its essential yet contested role in market-orientated, capitalist, liberal democracies around the world. The series reflects the multiple and inter-disciplinary forms PR takes in a post-Grunigian world; the expanding roles which it performs, and the increasing number of countries in which it is practised.

The series will examine current and explore new thinking on the key questions which impact upon PR and communications including:

- Is the evolution of persuasive communications in Central and Eastern Europe, China, Latin America, Japan, the Middle East and South East Asia developing new forms or following Western models?
- What has been the impact of postmodern sociologies, cultural studies and methodologies which are often critical of the traditional, conservative role of PR in capitalist political economies, and in patriarchy, gender and ethnic roles?
- What is the impact of digital social media on politics, individual privacy and PR practice? Is new technology changing the nature of content communicated, or simply reaching bigger audiences faster? Is digital PR a cause or a consequence of political and cultural change?

Books in this series will be of interest to academics and researchers involved in these expanding fields of study, as well as students undertaking advanced studies in this area.

Public Relations and Nation Building
Influencing Israel
Margalit Toledano and David McKie

Gender and Public Relations
Critical perspectives on voice, image and identity
Edited by Christine Daymon and Kristin Demetrious

Pathways to Public Relations
Histories of practice and profession
Edited by Burton Saint John III, Margot Opdycke Lamme and Jacquie L'Etang

Positioning Theory and Strategic Communications
A new approach to public relations research and practice
Melanie James

Public Relations and the History of Ideas
Simon Moore

Public Relations Ethics and Professionalism
The shadow of excellence
Johanna Fawkes

Power, Diversity and Public Relations
Lee Edwards

Power, Diversity and Public Relations

Lee Edwards

Routledge
Taylor & Francis Group

LONDON AND NEW YORK

First published 2015
by Routledge
2 Park Square, Milton Park, Abingdon, Oxon OX14 4RN

and by Routledge
711 Third Avenue, New York, NY 10017

Routledge is an imprint of the Taylor & Francis Group, an informa business

British Library Cataloguing in Publication Data
A catalogue record for this book is available from the British Library

Library of Congress Cataloging in Publication Data
Edwards, Lee (Lee M. S.)
Power, diversity and public relations / Lee Edwards.
pages cm. — (Routledge new directions in public relations and communication research)
Includes bibliographical references and index.
1. Public relations—Social aspects. 2. Public relations personnel.
3. Minorities. I. Title.
HM1221.E39 2014
659.2—dc23
2014009642

ISBN: 978-0-415-81195-8 (hbk)
ISBN: 978-0-203-06970-7 (ebk)

Typeset in Times New Roman
by Book Now Ltd, London

Printed and bound in the United States of America by
Edwards Brothers Malloy on sustainably sourced paper

For my family

Contents

Illustrations

Tables

Figure

Acknowledgements

One of the great privileges of academic life is the opportunity to immerse oneself in work that inspires, invigorates and directs one's thinking in unexpected ways. This book is a product of such opportunities, and I am grateful to those people whose scholarship has helped me think differently about power, diversity and PR. I hope I have done justice to their ideas.

Academia is also a social occupation; it is the conversations and seminars with colleagues that enable us to develop our own intellectual capacity, and I am lucky to have far too many people to thank for their contribution to what has transpired in these pages. Friends and colleagues in Leeds and elsewhere have provided encouragement, humour and inspiration, and without them I could not have completed the manuscript. Particular thanks must go to Clea Bourne, Stephen Coleman, Simon Gunn, Bob Heath, Alison Henderson, Dave Hesmondhalgh, Carrie Hodges, Helen Kennedy, Bethany Klein, Jacquie L'Etang, David McKie, Debashish Munshi, Daniel Muzio, Magda Pieczka, Ralph Tench, Liz Yeomans and Donnalyn Pompper, all of whom have been of seminal importance to the research and writing that made up this particular journey, whether they knew it or not.

I could not have begun to write about diversity in PR without the generosity of the participants, who shared their opinions, thoughts and stories so honestly and openly with me. I hope their voices are heard, and ultimately help to realize genuine change in the industry. My thanks go to all of them, and particularly to members of Ignite past and present, especially Bieneosa, Caroline, Magda, Paul, Sarah and Zena. Anamik Saha and Bieneosa Ebite receive special thanks for reading through the manuscript before its final submission and offering wise and helpful comments that have made this a better book. Routledge and Kevin Moloney have been endlessly patient during the process of putting this together, offering invaluable support.

Final thanks must go to my family, who 'wrote' this with me by virtue of the space, time and support they offered unconditionally. Bob, Marisa, Matt, Sally, Mitsu, Mia and A.G. – I hope you read it one day and think it was worth it!

1 Introduction

This book addresses the intransigent problem of improving the level of diversity in public relations. Since at least the early 1990s, the lack of diversity in the field has been recognized by academics and the need to broaden the range of people entering PR has been a regular, if minor theme for research. Practitioners too, have been prompted by legislative and social change to consider how they might open up their doors to people from a wider set of backgrounds and treat them equitably once they are included. 'Ethnic' communications has emerged as a PR specialism, with an increasing number of consultancies, and divisions within consultancies, set up to cater to the need to communicate with diverse communities (Weber Shandwick, 2007; Bourne, 2003).

However, this apparent integration has its limits. Ethnic communication is rarely integrated into mainstream PR strategies, and is instead treated as an adjunct to campaigns that take whiteness as the benchmark reference for messages and tactics (Bourne, 2003). Black, Asian and other minority ethnic (BAME) practitioners still only comprise 7 per cent of the industry (Wyatt, 2013), a significant under-representation given that the majority of the PR industry is located in London, where 40 per cent of the population is from non-white ethnic minority communities (Office for National Statistics, 2012). Informal and formal class distinctions remain a defining characteristic of the occupation, and while women dominate the occupation overall, men are still paid more and reach disproportionately higher levels of seniority (Wyatt, 2013; Edwards, 2008). In other words, PR is still very much an ethnically stratified industry, and is also marked by gender and class distinctions that are reminiscent of the advantageous subjectivities that men and members of the middle and upper class in the United Kingdom have historically enjoyed. Consequently, while BAME practitioners may be sought after as evidence of improved occupational diversity, or as a resource to connect with a valuable market, they remain 'outsiders-within' (Hill-Collins, 1990) the occupational field.

How are we to explain this? The formal criteria for entering PR are broad, rather than specific – and therefore perhaps more inclusive than exclusive. And it is not as if minority practitioners are not recognized: industry associations expound the benefits of improving diversity for business success. Something else must be going on.

I argue in this book that the reason diversity remains an issue in PR is to do with the ways in which the occupation itself operates. It is an institution that is driven to constantly legitimize its existence; the people within it must serve that purpose. The problem is that some people are perceived to be more useful than others in this endeavour, and those that are perceived to be less useful become marginalized. The process is implicit, hard to pin down, specify and combat. It is also invisible to those who 'fit' with what the occupation thinks it wants, who feel that their inclusion is part of the natural order of things. Processes of marginalization only become clear once the occupation is seen through the eyes of practitioners who experience them.

To put things a slightly different way, I am suggesting that the lack of diversity in PR is a result of the need to preserve occupational power. The latter is a function of the economic and social environment: occupations exist in competitive contexts, and people who join them enter with particular social, cultural and economic identities and assets that may be used to support the occupation's case for its existence. Once improving diversity is understood from this perspective, then assumptions that diversity will increase because targets are put in place, or because clients[1] want more diverse consultants, or because audiences are more diverse, become fragile. What really matters is whether a more diverse practitioner body, as the visible manifestation of the field's expertise, efficacy and talent, will reinforce the status of the occupation in relation to other competitive fields, and to those who lend it legitimacy (government and clients, for example). If the answer is no, the field will tend towards remaining largely homogenous.

And yet, that is not the whole story. The perspective I am adopting shifts the focus from numbers, or statistics, to struggles over the construction and valuation of identity. Identity is fluid, constantly being (re)constructed and a function of both structure and agency, not one or the other. Consequently, it is inaccurate to conceptualize 'diversity' as a static property of a field (although this is frequently done). It is better understood as a dynamic reality. While occupations may try to govern practice and identity in their own interests, individuals who are thereby marginalized find ways through the barriers they face and, very often, construct their desired careers regardless. In the subjectivities imposed upon them, are contained the clues that guide them to successfully challenge their liminal status, secure recognition and establish the right to belong in the field.

To fully understand how the issue of diversity (or rather, the lack of it) emerges, is experienced, and is sustained over time, we therefore need to investigate both sides of this dialectic: the structural and processual conditions that limit openness and the resistance of those who are 'othered' to systems of closure. This is the task I address in the following pages. Through a critical investigation of the occupational field, I aim to answer three fundamental questions about diversity in PR: In what ways does the occupation marginalize the lives and identities of ethnic minority practitioners? How does marginalization shape the experience of ethnic minority practitioners? And how do ethnic minority practitioners respond to marginalization as they pursue their careers?

I take 'race'[2] as my point of departure for analysing diversity in PR, although I regard identity as intersectional and how race articulates with class and gender is fundamental to the observations I make. Nonetheless, race is an important focus in its own right for three reasons. First, improving the racial diversity of the occupation has been an intermittent focus for the industry for some years (Chartered Institute of Public Relations (CIPR), 2013c, 2009b, 2006) and so this particular dimension of identity has clear relevance to the field. Second, focusing on race allowed me to manage the methodological difficulties presented by intersectionality, by offering a clear criteria for recruiting practitioners who were different in at least one dimension of their identity from the occupational norm (see Chapter 4 for a discussion of the normative occupational identity). But perhaps most importantly, race remains a marginalized area of concern in the field of the communications industries, and in PR in particular. We struggle to keep issues of race, racialization and racial discrimination on the scholarly and practitioner agenda, and this means that important and significant inequities are ignored. This study is one way of bringing such issues into the spotlight.

In this introductory chapter, I set out the key concepts and theoretical framework that underpin my argument as I elaborate it further in the rest of the book. I begin by reflecting on how diversity is treated in policy and practice, before considering the conceptualizations of identity, race and racism that underpin the book. For those who have studied the sociology of occupations, many of the points I make will be familiar. However, they have yet to be integrated fully into an understanding of the way diversity issues have evolved in PR. This book is an opportunity to set out such an understanding, and perhaps push diversity scholarship and practice in PR into a wider, more creative arena.

Diversity in policy and practice

To put the subject of this book in context, it is important to understand how and why 'diversity' has been treated as a matter of political and economic concern. To begin with, how might we define 'diversity' within PR? Who counts as diverse? We all differ from each other in different ways, so it could be regarded as nonsensical to speak of improving diversity, since diversity exists across the human race, and managing diversity then becomes a matter of maximizing individual potential (Noon, 2007). Ely and Thomas (2001) suggest that managing diversity is a means of differentiating groups, usually based on demographic characteristics, and note the importance of power dynamics as underlying factors in how diversity is perceived and understood in organizations. Given that articulations of difference are fundamentally about the relative power of different subjectivities (Flintoff *et al.*, 2008), a productive starting point for investigations of diversity in PR would be one that foregrounds diversity as an important dimension of power, a political issue. Rather than asking who counts as diverse, we might better ask *who is disadvantaged or privileged* by virtue of their identity?

In fact, this formulation does not take us much further on: we could all argue that aspects of our identity disadvantage us at some time in some way. However, questions of diversity in occupations and organizations are important because they address *systemic* disadvantage, not the occasional difficult experience. To be more specific in this context, the question of 'who counts' might become 'who is systematically disadvantaged or privileged, across different social institutions, by virtue of their identity?'. Anthias (2001) suggests that we should consider the primary social definers of gender, race and class when analysing disadvantage. Other aspects of identity may also generate discrimination, but to avoid the trap (and analytical nightmare) of endless proliferation, gender, race and class can be justifiably prioritized as the 'primary organizing principles of a society which locates and positions groups within that society's opportunity structures' (Zinn and Thornton Dill, 1996: 322–323). In PR, diversity research has traditionally addressed discrimination facing women and ethnic minorities (Daymon and Demetrious, 2013, 2010; Aldoory, 2007; Aldoory and Toth, 2002; Hon and Brunner, 2000) as well as, more recently, class (Waymer, 2012), sexuality (Tindall and Waters, 2012) and age (Pompper, 2013).

Diversity as disadvantage is commonly treated as a matter about which something should be 'done'. It is a locus for action, both imagined – strategies should improve diversity at some point in the future – and real – we implement policies and practices that are, in themselves, changes in the present. It is, as Ahmed (2012) argues, both a performative term and a performance. It 'does' things, it prompts doing, and it is a way of being seen to do things. In this sense, diversity initiatives serve the interests of organizations as much as (if not more than) those of the individuals they are supposed to serve and frequently do little to change fundamental relations of power (Johns and Green, 2009; Creegan *et al.*, 2003; Webb, 1997). From a societal perspective, diversity is also pragmatic: 'more' diversity leads to other good things: a larger share of the national economic pie, social mobility and its attendant benefits such as better education, inherited wealth and happier and more engaged citizens.

Managing diversity is neither simple nor necessarily productive – diversity initiatives have been around for a long time in different guises and, in PR and other professional and semi-professional occupations, not a lot has changed (Professional Associations Research Network, 2010; The Panel on Fair Access to the Professions, 2009). Speaking about diversity, managing diversity or improving diversity in occupations, then, is to engage with a complex problematic operating on a number of levels. However, at face value the word diversity itself suggests numerical variety, and many industry and policy initiatives relating to 'improving diversity' tend to suggest that numerical improvements are a desired outcome. If diversity is about numbers, then improving diversity can be realized by improving access to formerly exclusive occupations: attracting *more* people, and making it easier for them to enter and remain in the field, will ensure 'diversity' is realized.

Improving access is most frequently interpreted as structural reform. For example, in the United Kingdom, equal opportunities legislation has outlawed explicit discrimination across a range of social categories (Equality Act, 2010) and government endorsement of widening participation initiatives in the Higher Education (HE) sector continues. The corresponding growth in the number of highly qualified women and ethnic minority individuals, has indeed facilitated their participation in professional workforces (Atewologun and Singh, 2010;

Muzio and Ackroyd, 2005; Davidson and Burke, 2004; Sommerlad and Sanderson, 1998). Occupations across the board have responded to the impetus of government policy with programmes to address diversity as a means of playing their part in efforts to distribute economic and cultural wealth more evenly throughout the population (Muzio and Tomlinson, 2012; British Medical Association, 2009; Farmbrough, 2009; The Law Society, 2009; Arts Council England, 2008). Meanwhile, organizations enthusiastically adopt diversity management policies as a means of realizing business interests, remaining competitive in a diverse market and tapping into the 'brown', 'pink' or 'grey' pound.

However, improving diversity is not simply a question of manipulating a mathematical equation. A second important assumption underpinning diversity initiatives is that if occupations make it easier for 'different' people to join *and work* in their fields, diversity will happen. Thus, improving and managing diversity involves acknowledging the different life circumstances of those who differ from the standard professional, the 'unencumbered (white) man' (Acker, 2006: 450) and the ways in which the structures of occupational fields work against their participation.[3] To paraphrase a well-known movie line, it is a matter of 'if you build it *in the right way*, they will come'. Diversity should grow, once encouraged through changes to access *and* structural working conditions.

In normative PR research on diversity, the idea of 'counting' diversity is reflected in the notion of requisite variety, where the level of diversity in the profession is determined by the variety of audiences that need to be addressed (Sha and Ford, 2007; Hon and Brunner, 2000; Dozier and Broom, 1995; Grunig, 1992). The assumption is that communication is enhanced when receivers can relate in some way to the sender (Perloff, 1993) and while 'matching' PR professionals with the characteristics of their audiences may not be required, an ability to understand the world in which those audiences live is necessary if communication is to be effective (Holtzhausen, 2012; Sriramesh and Verčič, 2009; Sriramesh, 2002; Banks, 2000). Given this apparent enthusiasm for the business case, it is no surprise that the industry has implemented various policy initiatives to address the problem of diversity in PR, improve access and increase the numbers of ethnic minority practitioners working in the field (see, for example, Public Relations Consultants Association (PRCA), 2013a; CIPR, 2012).

In PR, entry criteria (broadly, a good undergraduate degree and some experience in the industry) have remained largely unchanged, perhaps because they are already relatively open. Only one recruitment-related area has prompted significant attention: that of unpaid internships, with a campaign initiated by the PRCA to ensure that all hopeful graduates have a chance to gain valuable on-the-job experience, not just those few whose families can afford to subsidize them while they work for free (PR Week, 2013b; PRCA, 2013b).[4] For the most part, in fact, a brief review of diversity policies reveals that 'improving diversity' has become a matter of addressing wider issues of practice and process in recruitment and progression. These include altering recruitment processes so that a wider pool of applicants are seen; ensuring equity in pay, promotion and career opportunities; and promoting flexible working practices.

The rhetoric surrounding such initiatives is celebratory: diversity policies are couched in terms that emphasize the benefits of a diverse society, and the value that integrating diversity can bring to the occupation. Diversity is a Good Thing. In the United Kingdom, for example, both the CIPR and the PRCA have instituted comprehensive diversity policies and established formal working groups.

> The CIPR is committed to improving diversity and equality as an integral part of all its activity. In addition, we aim to ensure that the PR Industry is aware that we all work in a richly diverse society, and that the profession can benefit from diversity. Ultimately our aim is to have diversity embedded in public relations activity and recognized as a core resource for the industry.
>
> (CIPR, 2009b)

> The Diversity Network works to open up access to the communications profession and make it more representative of the nation. [...]
>
> Tanya [Josephs, Chair of the Diversity Network] said: 'I believe that the question of diversity will be integral to the success or failure of the PR industry in the next five years. Only with a workforce that is truly representative of the nation will we be taken seriously. This is a call to arms and we challenge PRCA members who want to see this happen to join our Network and get involved in enabling the next generation of PR talent'.
>
> (PRCA, 2013a)

Such statements are a powerful recognition that the industry itself needs to be educated and recognize the importance of diversity, indeed that diversity is a matter of occupational life and death. They place the onus on the occupational field, rather than the 'diverse' individual, to make a difference to diversity. However, rhetoric is easily constructed, particularly by PR experts; what matters is the extent to which such ambitions are realized, or, alternatively, the extent to which they constitute an 'empty shell' that generates little significant change (Hoque and Noon, 2004).

Some practical changes in working conditions have emerged. Part-time working, job sharing and flexible working are now common practice in many occupations, and certainly in PR. But no matter how much of a Good Thing diversity is, and no matter how skilful the rhetoric, a lack of diversity remains an intractable problem for the industry. Diversity in PR in the United Kingdom has increased only marginally, from 6 per cent to 7 per cent in eight years, and with a slight decrease over the last two years (Wyatt, 2013; PR Week/PRCA, 2011; Centre for Economics and Business Research Ltd., 2005). At that rate, we would have to wait another 30 years before the level reached just 20 per cent – and even this would still be only half the current level of diversity in the population of London and the South East, where the majority of the UK industry is located (Office for National Statistics, 2012). Diversity policies are clearly not as effective as they might be. Perhaps, as Ahmed (2007b) found in her study of higher education, demonstrating diversity has become a simple matter of setting out a policy for PR practitioners and recruiters. Perhaps the existence of the policy eases the pressure to take genuine and concrete action that will produce lasting change.[5] Indeed, diversity policies can be *non*-performative: merely the act of articulating them confirms that we are serious about diversity, and they need not generate other forms of action (Ahmed, 2012, 2007a).

Part of the problem lies in the fact that diversity initiatives underpinned by business rationales fail to address the systemic disadvantage that derives from historical prejudice and discrimination (see Chapter 2) because they are grounded in the needs of organizations in the present and largely separated from any sense of political, moral or rights-based argument to recognize and remedy systemic discrimination (Faist, 2009; Ahmed, 2007a). As Noon (2007) has pointed out, 'diversity' as commonly used in organizational contexts, is designed to achieve organizational, rather than societal objectives, such as higher financial returns, or a more effective service delivery (Faist, 2009). It is characterized by Western, individualized modes of thinking about difference and hybridity that ultimately take refuge in the idea of original, 'pure' racial groupings, rather than making space for alternative, more dynamic discourses of identity (Hutnyk, 2006; Munshi and Kurian, 2005; Munshi and McKie, 2001). This 'diminishes the significance of ethnic identity by trivializing it and overlooking the negative impact of some social group characteristics (such as ethnicity) on employment' (Noon, 2007: 774). The focus instead is on finding ways to realize the financial or other organizational benefits that diversity can deliver.

An ahistorical and amoral business rationale also means that 'managing diversity' easily morphs from an initiative aimed at supporting particular individuals to a means of delivering competitive advantage.[6] In this transformation the rhetoric of inclusion that underpins celebratory statements is revealed to be a fiction. 'Managing' diversity turns diversity into an object, rather than an aspect of identity; managing diversity is a strategy and set of tactics to manage the 'object' that is diverse. As Faist (2009: 178) notes, diversity is 'the perceived, evaluated form of (cultural) difference' (my emphasis). Somewhat ironically, the result is that policies ostensibly designed to advance the status of 'other' practitioners, instead position them squarely as economic assets to be manipulated for economic gain. They oscillate between being hyper-visible (when useful) and invisible (when not required) (Puwar, 2004). For BAME PR practitioners in the United Kingdom, the position is not so far removed from that of their ancestors in the days of Empire (see Chapter 2). And like those ancestors, the economic justification for their employment makes them dispensable. If the costs of employing them become greater than the returns, the assets they bring to an organization may be sought elsewhere, or simply jettisoned (Carbado and Gulati, 2003). In the business case for diversity, there is no alternative rationale for inclusion (Noon, 2007).

Moreover, the business rationale for diversity works to silence the 'other'. To embody diversity means to be 'added on' to a (white, middle-class, male, heterosexual) institutional body, an unequivocally positive event (for the institution) that demands the 'diverse' individual demonstrate their pleasure at being included (Ahmed, 2009). Being included is an achievement that co-opts the individual on the side of those who claim racism and racialization have been somehow overcome: the 'other' must 'authorize the universality of Whiteness by identifying with it' (Sharma and Sharma, 2003: 307). As a result, histories of inequity and their legacies in the present remain unspoken, for fear of disturbing the imaginary fabric of 'happy diversity' (Ahmed, 2009). Nothing fundamental is required to shift, other than the way the way the institution is perceived: 'diversity becomes about changing perceptions of whiteness rather than changing the whiteness of organizations' (Ahmed, 2009: 45). Speaking out about the continued existence of racism despite 'diversity' would transform the 'other's' status from being an asset to a problem for the institution.

In summary, diversity research and practice shows that diversity is understood by policymakers, industry associations and organizations as an important issue, but when envisaged as structural issues of access and working conditions in the context of the business case, diversity policies have had only limited effects. The slow progress of diversity in PR suggests that the industry is no exception to this rule. Moreover, there are no penalties associated with lack of progress, suggesting that in fact, *not* doing anything about diversity might be more acceptable than diversity policies imply. Once we consider the wider, less positive effects of the business case on the identity and participation of the 'other' in the workplace, such a state of affairs is easier to understand.

In fact, the justification for addressing diversity in the occupation, and for caring about whether it exists or not, is much more fundamental than being a matter of business sense, commercial advantage or individual equity – although all these ideas play into why diversity in the workplace merits our attention and concern. In fact, occupational diversity is an expression of the quality of democracy that we nurture in the spaces where people enact crucial dimensions of their lives. Once we take diversity to be a democratic initiative, different questions arise about the quality and extent of participation that the 'other' is permitted. Presence does not equate to participation. The 'other' must be allowed to speak, too, and in speaking, must be able to construct a narrative of the world that reflects their own experience, rather than being required to reflect mainstream interpretations of reality. As Couldry (2010: 100) notes, the ability to give account of oneself is a basic right: 'The denial of [the narratable self] is a fundamental denial of someone's status as human'. Perhaps most importantly, the narratives that the 'other' contributes must be recognized as being of value, part of the process of social exchange that defines our (working) lives. In other words, it is not enough for diverse voices in PR to speak into an occupational vacuum. Their narratives must be taken account of, interacted with, and recognized as a form of agency that has the capacity to generate change (Couldry, 2010: 7–9). Diversity initiatives, then, should be a means for the redistribution of occupational power by attaching value to 'other' voices, or making sure they 'matter' in the field.[7] It is in this sense that I argue for diversity to be understood as an expression of democracy.

Intersectionality, disadvantage and privilege

If diversity is about democracy, then the institutional view of diversity can only reflect one dimension of the dynamics of power with which diversity initiatives engage. I noted in the introduction that difference as hierarchy is grounded in valuing identity in particular ways. The politics of diversity begin with these valuations; they provide the logic for giving some people 'voice' and preventing 'others' from speaking. In other words, the normally subdued voices and experiences of marginalized individuals are also essential to understanding how and why diversity is not only a Good Thing, but also a political matter. In the context of a neoliberal business environment where *dissolving* difference is often the preferred approach to diversity (Liff, 1997), voicing alternative positions 'challenges the silences and gaps that arise when decisions on one scale – the market functioning – seem naturally to 'trump' the potential exercise of voice on other scales' (Couldry, 2010: 13). Making space for 'other' voices and discourses is a way of validating 'other' experiences, in an environment where the availability of normative language to express such experiences may be limited.

To understand identity politics, we must complicate the gender, race and class categories that Anthias suggests can direct our research by recognizing that identity is intersectional: gender, race and class do not generate separate forms of disadvantage that somehow operate in parallel. They are entwined and mutually constitutive, each affecting the meaning of the other, with effects that vary across different contexts and for different individuals (Walby, 2007; Crenshaw, 1991; Hill-Collins, 1990; King, 1988). Intersectionality is an important, disruptive approach to identity that challenges hegemonic occupational discourses and practices by introducing and validating 'other' voices and experiences (Dhamoon, 2011; Vardeman-Winter and Tindall, 2010; Holvino, 2008; Valentine, 2007). It prompts researchers to beware of simplistic and essentializing work and instead recognize the complex impact of social categorization on people's daily lives (Jordan-Zachery, 2007; Davis, 2008). The term was first coined by Kimberle Crenshaw (1989), a critical race scholar whose work echoed black feminist arguments that the diversity of female experience should be recognized in scholarly literature and policymaking (Yuval-Davis, 2006; Brah and Phoenix, 2004; Hill-Collins, 1990; King, 1988). She introduced the idea of 'intersectionality' to account for the experiences of black women in the United States, who faced unique disadvantages as a result of their gender and race. Taking the idea a step further, Hill-Collins (1990) called the interlocking systems of class, gender and racial disadvantage a 'matrix of domination', creating unique experiences at the personal, community and institutional levels. Since these beginnings, scholars have tried to add depth to intersectionality as a theoretical and analytical paradigm for generating research that can enable communities to mobilize and change the status quo (Bilge, 2010).

Revealing the complexity of daily life for marginalized groups remains central to intersectionality work. Certainly, at a macro-level it is clear that individuals subject to multiple disadvantageous social categorizations are vulnerable to distinct forms of inequity (Penner and Saperstein, 2013; Carastathis, 2008; Steinbugler *et al.*, 2006; Mynatt *et al.*, 1997). On the other hand, narrative investigations of lived experience treat the individual as a locus of intersectionality; in these studies, the meanings associated with social categories are contested and intersesctionality only becomes meaningful through the conduit of individual lives (Vardeman-Winter and Tindall, 2010; Hulko, 2009; Valentine, 2007; Adib and Guerrier, 2003; Trethewey, 1997). These studies reflect an interpretation of intersectionality at the micro-level and de-centre categories by emphasizing the fact that difference is located within, rather than between identities (Fuss, 1989: 103).

The importance of institutional manifestations of intersectionality and its embeddedness across society has driven more recent theorizations of intersectionality. Walby (2007: 454), for example, argues that intersectional scholarship must take into account the 'full ontological depth' of race, gender and class, as 'sets of social relations [...] not flattened to a culturally reductionist concept of identity, or economically reductionist concept of class'. Instead, she suggests, recognizing their ontological depth means recognizing them as 'overlapping, non-saturating and non-nested systems' that are 'constituted in the institutional domains of economy, polity, violence and civil society'. Walby's approach is echoed by Holvino (2008: 249), who suggests intersections should be conceptualized as 'simultaneous processes of identity, institutional and social practice', while Winker and Degele (2011: 54) define intersectionality as the interactions between social structures, symbolic representations and identity constructions. Yuval-Davis (2006: 198) and Anthias (2013: 10) suggest that the material and symbolic use of race, gender and class categories to construct division and difference, advantage and disadvantage in particular situations, should be examined from a relational perspective on four levels: organizational – the structures and processes of specific institutions; intersubjective – the formal and informal interactions between people; experiential – the subjective experience of daily life for individuals; and representational – the different ideological means of representing and associating value with difference.

Importantly for white-collar occupations like PR, where all practitioners benefit from relatively high levels of cultural and economic capital, Hill-Collins (1990: 225) argues that intersectionality 'opens up possibilities for a "both/and" conceptual stance, one in which all groups possess varying amounts of penalty and privilege in one historically created system'. It allows us to recognize that privilege can co-exist with disadvantage; for example, a black PR practitioner from a middle-class family in the United Kingdom may suffer from marginalization less often than their black, working-class colleague, and might actively use their class status to offset the disadvantage of their racial identity. In other words, individuals can negotiate their position by re-defining their identity in ways that counter their disadvantage. This active, 'strategic intersectionality' (Fraga *et al.*, 2006) is grounded in reflexivity and an awareness of self/other that those who occupy liminal spaces in society, as 'outsiders-within' institutional contexts, inevitably develop (Ladson-Billings, 2000).

Intersectionality underlines the fact that identity is social, as well as individual, historically determined as well as individually negotiated. It reinforces the idea of identity as always under construction, as Hall (1996) notes, and the conditions of its construction are partly historical: we are all subject to certain 'conditions of arrival' that accompany us into different locations (Ahmed, 2006) producing stereotypical preconceptions about our abilities and our right to belong. The body is an important medium for this interaction. While the meanings attached to a body may be variable (see below), the body itself is ineradicable (Fuss, 1989). As such, it occupies the role of 'signifier of the condensation of subjectivities in the individual' over time (Hall, 1996: 11). In other words, the bodies of women, ethnic minority and working class individuals still carry resonances of the inferior position that they have historically occupied in relation to white, middle- and upper-class men. That position shapes the way they are perceived in the workplace today, by furnishing normative subjectivities, stereotypes that are never accurate, but nonetheless predetermine who they 'are' at the point of arrival in different spaces and places (Ahmed, 2000; Coates, 2008). Should they enter spaces where their normative identity (e.g. as a Black woman, or an Indian man) would not normally place them, their presence causes surprise and fear. More often than not, their colleagues manage this unease by orienting away from them, constructing their difference from the norm as a negative and marginalizing them in more or less subtle ways (Ahmed, 2006; Puwar, 2004).

Because 'condensed subjectivities' are a product of history, we always carry them with us. However, they do not over-determine our experience; on the contrary, as intersectionality research suggests, we negotiate them. We might partially or fully conform to them. We might reinterpret or reject them. Our position is dependent on the situation, and therefore the nature of disadvantage – and the potential for resistance – is also context-dependent (Gunaratnam, 2003). The choices we make are determined by variable interactions of experience, structural position, and specific historical and social circumstances that constitute different situations (Werbner, 2013; Hancock, 2007; Brah, 1992). As we make those choices, we (re)create our identity in a fluid and ongoing dialectical process, as a 'temporary attachment to subject positions' (Hall, 1996: 4) that offers the flexibility to respond to stereotypes in ways that are most productive for particular situations. Nonetheless, while new possibilities for constructing identity are always emerging, it is a permanent possibility that we have 'the abjections of [our] embodiment re-imposed' (Sommerlad, 2009: 176) in each new environment we enter. Herein lies the systemic nature of disadvantage. It is a product of history, as much as the present. And while we can re-negotiate the present, we cannot change the past.

The language of diversity management exacerbates the problem. Essentialized identities provide the rationale for targeting certain individuals (in crude terms, 'we need more African PR practitioners to connect better with African communities'/'we need more working-class PR practitioners to connect better with working-class communities'). The organizational disconnect from the wider social and cultural context (a multicultural rather than monocultural world), means such identities are reified, and the lines drawn between 'us' and 'them' as an simplistic, uncomplicated 'other', remain intact (Zanoni and Janssens, 2004). Intersectionality is not acknowledged and consequently diversity discourses do little to disturb either stereotypes about the 'other' or existing organizational hierarchies. Intersectionality, on the other hand, challenges the assumptions that frame much diversity research and practice, in PR and elsewhere. It refutes essentialism; in recognizing the power to 'speak back' to institutions, organizations and individuals who prefer to silence 'other' voices, it 'changes dominant organizational [and, I would argue, occupational] narratives that privilege the experience of white men and women and construct organizations within the liberal paradigm of maleness, heterosexism, whiteness and western-ness' (Holvino, 2008: 16).

Focusing on identity as a complex outcome of social relations means that no one variable can be used to define diversity, nor will the management of one, narrowly defined group of people resolve the issues a lack of diversity presents. Nor can the sets of social relations that characterize occupations like PR, constructed through gender, race, class or other social categorization, be treated separately, or as parallel systems of disadvantage. There is no 'magic bullet' (Hancock, 2007) that will resolve inequality. We must consider how personal and collective experience, knowledge and subjectivity can be used as a powerful resource to resist discrimination, since intersectionality applies as much to domination as it does to subjugation (Levine-Rasky, 2011). As soon as we consider one dimension of identity, we must, by definition, consider its relation to others as well (Brah, 1992), and beware of reifying disadvantage at the expense of recognizing the ways that gender, race and class can also produce privilege.

Racialization and whiteness

Intersectionality underpins the approach I take to identity in this book, in that I understand the experience of diversity to be complex and driven by multiple dimensions of identity simultaneously. However, I take race as my analytical starting point. As I noted in the introduction, race has been neglected in the field of PR and communications studies more widely, and putting it at the centre of this study facilitates a long-overdue examination of 'the damage that racisms are still doing to democracy' (Gilroy, 2004: 35) in the context of working lives. Just as race itself has always been political (see Chapter 2), centring race is a political decision that reveals both the 'alchemical power' (Gilroy, 2004: 34) of racism to transform symbolic and material violence into a normative world, and the fictions that it produces in the process.

Race and racism have specific, material and symbolic forms and effects that cannot be reduced to other aspects of identity. Race is 'a structure of power, a focus of political struggle and hence a fundamental force in shaping women's and men's lives' (Zinn and Thornton Dill, 1996: 324). Following Munshi and Edwards (2011), I am interpreting race not as an individual, essential or biological attribute, but as 'a process of structured events which over time demonstrate a system whereby groups and individuals are racialized' (Coates,

2006: 5). The accommodation of time is crucial; in a 'post-race' society, racism can rarely be pinned down as a cause of individual events, but over time, patterns of meaning that reflect the centrality of race to disadvantage or marginalization bear testament to its continued existence and influence. The covert racism that results emerges through the meanings associated with structured events – for example, PR recruitment or promotion processes across recruitment specialists, consultancies or in-house (Coates, 2008). Meaning is fluid and contextual, rather than fixed, but the condensed subjectivities that our bodies inhere lead to a degree of regularity in the meanings associated with our race, as well as our class and gender, across different times and places, resulting in systems of racialization that increase the likelihood that racial elites will be more successful than non-elites. In other words, racialization is 'ordinary' rather than exceptional, institutionalized and shaped by history (Carbado and Gulati, 2013; Coates, 2008; Cole, 2004; Delgado and Stefancic, 2001).

The nature of racialization differs depending on the circumstances that surround its emergence (Zinn and Thornton Dill, 1996). The experience of PR practitioners of colour in the United States, for example, is in part determined by the historical meanings associated with being Black, Asian or Latina in the US context, while for UK practitioners, the history of Empire and post-colonial immigration is more pertinent to the racialization they experience (Sommerlad, 2008a; Cole, 2004; Hall, 1988b; Gilroy, 1987). Similarly, racialization in the legal profession will differ from racialization in the field of PR. Racialization may therefore be understood as located, rather than generalizable (Schueller, 2009). In a globalized world, however, locatedness does not equate to isolation. Systems connect across local, national and global geographies (Giddens, 1999; Bauman, 1998; Appadurai, 1996), so that different, but connected forms of racialization and racism will emerge across time and place (Said, 1994). They are also fluid, rather than fixed; the disadvantage of some racialized groups always exists in relation to the privilege enjoyed by others, and this relational connection means that any movement on either side generates a response in its opposite. In fact, Debashish Munshi and I have argued elsewhere (Munshi and Edwards, 2011) that PR is part of wider systems of racialization, complicit in the perpetuation of privilege and disadvantage affecting different racialized groups, not least because practitioners deploy race as a static, simplistic variable to categorize audiences, practitioners, messages and campaigns in ways that assume consistent and predictable identities across time and space.

Whiteness is a particularly important form of racialization, a socially constructed system of ideological categorizations that shape the life experiences of those who are White and those who are not (McKinney, 2005; McIntosh, 1997). Whiteness is inextricably linked to the 'others' (those who do not count as white) against which it defines itself; it cannot be sustained without its counterpoint (McIntyre, 1997). In the US and UK contexts, whiteness operates in different ways because it is shaped by different histories, but in both cases whiteness acts as a form of property, allowing those who possess it access to wider and greater forms of institutional, organizational and individual privilege than those who cannot claim it (Puwar, 2004; Carbado and Gulati, 2003; McIntosh, 1997; Harris, 1993). Whiteness has great resilience, operating in ways that protect its sovereignty. For example, while civil rights movements have been successful in ensuring that overt racism is now illegal in the USA and the United Kingdom, analyses show that more subtle forms of racism continue to exist and that the notion of Whiteness as a form of property that leads to privilege has remained intact (Harris, 1993). Progress against racism, then, is only achievable if a form of interest convergence is at work (Bell, 1980); that is, when taking steps to reduce discrimination is in the interest of both dominant (normally white) and subordinated (normally non-white) groups. The business case for diversity in PR, for example, may be understood as a theoretical and practical discourse of interest convergence (we welcome 'others' because 'others' help us communicate more effectively).

In associating particular meanings with race, gender, class and other social categories, whiteness produces normative subjectivities for individuals in terms of, for example, their criminality, intelligence, creativity, athleticism or other attributes, that have a material effect on their experiences in social institutions such as education, the legal system, or indeed their occupational field (Hylton, 2009; Gillborn, 2008; Gray and Leith, 2004; Bagilhole and Goode, 2001; Frankenberg, 1993; Hill-Collins, 1990). These subjectivities also form the basis of judgements about suitability for different occupations: Black men may be perceived to be more suited to a career in IT, for example, than a career in finance or PR, while white men may be more readily understood as embodying leadership potential (Logan, 2011). As Ladson-Billings (1999: 9) argues: 'In a society where whiteness is positioned as normative everyone is ranked and categorized in relation to these points of opposition. These categories fundamentally sculpt the extant terrain of possibilities even when other possibilities exist'. Importantly, the privilege associated with whiteness is usually invisible to those who inhabit or possess it; it is, however, highly visible to those whom it 'others' (Shome, 2000).

While my approach to race and racialization perhaps emphasizes structures and systems, they are not static, but are understood as a potential locus for change, as long as existing institutional norms can be disrupted. As discussed, disruption is prompted by making visible previously hidden identities and voices; their narratives interrupt accepted truths (Shome and Hedge, 2002) and reveal where the modern-day 'colour-line' lies (DuBois, 1903). Hearing the voices of marginalized groups is especially important in locations where their knowledge, experience and interpretations of a particular institutional or societal context have previously been ignored (Crenshaw, 1991; Spivak, 1988). Occupational fields are examples of such locations, where normative white, male, middle-class, heterosexual identities are reflected in practices that privilege the social, economic and cultural forms of capital that white, straight middle-class men are able to claim (Kyriacou and Johnston, 2011; Anderson-Gough *et al.*, 2005; Grey, 1998; Kay and Hagan, 1998; Witz, 1992). 'Other' narratives show how racialization emerges, reveal implicit divisions and mechanisms of inclusion and exclusion that divide those who belong and those who don't, those who may speak and those who are silenced, and those who can choose their own path from those whose choices are limited by the meaning attached to their identities. They also demonstrate how marginalized members of the field can contest and change its parameters (Muzio and Tomlinson, 2012). In such contexts, providing a space for marginalized voices through research is an empowering process (Gunaratnam, 2003). Practitioners who participated in this study, for example, commented on the importance of having a forum where they could speak freely, and where their experiences and opinions would be heard and valued. Marginalized voices also reveal important insights derived from the experience of living and working in a 'liminal space' of alterity (Ladson-Billings and Donnor, 2008; Ladson-Billings, 2000), always fitting in and never truly 'self' or 'other'. They illustrate the ways that 'others' are perceived by dominant groups, the 'othering' that is constructed through ideologies such as whiteness, but also the power that liminal knowledge affords, because it allows them to understand and undermine the logic of whiteness, thus expanding the possibilities available to them within a field (Rollock, 2012).

A framework for analysis

I draw on these theoretical insights about identity, race and racialization to frame my exploration of the dialectics of power and diversity in the UK PR industry. This means temporally and historically locating the field and its practitioners, investigating processes rather than categories, and complicating, rather than simplifying, the occupational field. I adopt a dialectical analytical approach (Martin and Nakayama, 1999) that highlights the fluid relationship between the PR field and its Black, Asian and other minority ethnic (BAME) practitioners. My focus is on the changing connections between constructions of identity, race as process and the occupational field to reveal how power in PR continually moves between insiders and outsiders-within (Hill-Collins, 1990), is bound to the past and shapes the future.

I am guided by the four dialectics proposed by Munshi and Edwards (2011), and ask the following specific questions in the context of each:

- *Racialized elites/racialized non-elites.* How are elites and non-elites constructed by the occupational field, and on what basis is this contested by BAME practitioners? What kinds of structured events result in race becoming a meaningful criterion for membership of either group? How do other aspects of identity interact with race to facilitate inclusion in or exclusion from either group? And when, how and on what basis do practitioners move between the two groups?
- *Visible/invisible.* Whose knowledge and presence is acknowledged by the occupational field and by BAME practitioners? Whose is obscured? What kinds of structured events give rise to this visibility/invisibility? How does the absence of some voices and the presence of others produce particular racialized subjectivities for different individuals? How does giving voice to otherwise invisible perspectives of PR affect the dominant narratives of 'truth' about the field, its identity and the identity of its practitioners.

- *Process/category*. In the context of what kinds of structured events does the idea of race, as used by the occupational field and BAME practitioners, move between process and category? How do race-as-process and race-as-category coexist or conflict in different discourses, practices and interactions? How does this movement change the power available to BAME practitioners and their white colleagues?
- *General/particular*. When and how is the management of BAME practitioners marked by generalizations and/or specifics? What effect does this have on their occupational power and how does this affect the strategies they use for resistance?

Answering these questions means analysing domination and resistance, privilege and disadvantage at the organizational, intersubjective, representational and experiential levels of PR work, as Yuval-Davis (2006) suggests. I return to them in the conclusion, where I consider how the evidence from the study can enlighten our understanding of each one in the context of the aforementioned dialectical engagements. In broad terms, I argue that diversity in the occupational field of PR in the United Kingdom can only be fully understood through an analysis of the interactions between the racialization of BAME practitioners produced by a form of occupational whiteness specific to the history of PR and racism in this country, and the responses of BAME practitioners to these imposed subjectivities, marked by reinterpretations of normative discourses and practices in ways that empower, rather than subjugate, their identities, and assert their right to belong. I do not wish to fall into the trap of essentializing identities, and my argument is not that all BAME practitioners will inevitably experience discrimination, nor that all white practitioners enjoy privilege. On the contrary, many participants in the study told of situations where race was irrelevant to their work. My argument is rather, that the racialization that permeates PR, which normalizes whiteness over other identities, makes BME practitioners permanently vulnerable to marginalization, and that they manage this threat on an ongoing basis, even if it does not transpire in every interaction they have with the field.

Positioning myself in the study

Hill-Collins (1990: 236) argues that 'partiality and not universality is the condition of being heard; individuals and groups forwarding knowledge claims without owning their position are deemed less credible than those who do'. As a white, middle-class female academic with Irish and Welsh heritage, my background clearly differed from my participants. My motivation to investigate the issue of diversity in PR came from an instinctive desire for social justice, something that my parents instilled in me from a young age, as activist Catholics very much engaged with the Church's social teaching (although not with its restrictive, discriminatory prescriptions about individual lives). They demonstrated for the anti-apartheid movement, for the Campaign for Nuclear Disarmament and for peace in the Middle East, they joined and used their trade unions, and as we got older, we were encouraged to do the same.

I grew up in a white Irish community in the northwest of England, and encountered few people of colour during my childhood or teenage years; at university, my cohort was also all white, with the exception of one black student. However, I had always had an interest in culture and difference, studying languages and travelling before, during and after university. My first substantial experience of the complexities of difference based on race and ethnicity came relatively late, when I moved to New Zealand in my twenties as the newly married wife of a New Zealand Samoan. The differences between us were classed, gendered and raced. As a Pacific Islander in New Zealand, he was 'othered' on the basis of his race, while I was accepted. The places he took us to socialize in were working class (pubs and working men's clubs) in contrast to the middle-class theatre and live gigs I initiated. His friends were more diverse (in terms of class and race) than mine, who I had met while studying for an MPhil when I first moved there. He worked as a barman and builder, while I was headed for a professional career. He earned less than I did once I was out of college, which reversed our traditionally gendered roles within the marriage and affected my potential role as a mother (at the time, New Zealand did not have statutory maternity leave, so having children was a complicated financial juggling act). The latter compromised our (already complicated) identity as a 'couple' in the eyes of his family, who were expecting us to live close by and have children sooner rather than later. He felt out of place among my intellectual friends, while my white privilege meant I felt I had the right to belong with his family and friends. His family and community traditions remained strong, while my identity was somewhat vague, independent of community and anchored to little other than my immediate family. We lived and negotiated these differences on an ongoing basis, but it was the first time in my life that I experienced what it meant to be an outsider-within. My husband rarely felt completely comfortable in my circle of friends, while my sense of difference from his family never left me, even after years of marriage. I have not forgotten the feeling of unease that comes with being out of place, even when, in formal terms, one can legitimately claim a place. It continues to inform my research and is the root of the question that prompted this empirical study: 'what is it like to be "different" from the norm in the PR industry?'

Researching race 'runs the risk of reifying the very thing we are seeking to deny' (Alexander, 2006: 403), and in the study, my desire not to make my participants feel out of place, nor to essentialize or pigeonhole them as victims, meant I was initially cautious about even raising the issue of race and racism, and instead phrased questions in broad terms of 'difference'. I was also conscious of the power dynamics inherent in doing research about race and ethnicity that runs the risk of privileging the researcher's status and interpretation, while essentializing and objectifying participants' lives and identities in the service of the academy (Gunaratnam, 2003). Here, the risk is that the research subject disappears, their ontology and epistemology is colonized by the academy and their voices are occluded (Alexander, 2006). My initial reaction to this danger was to disappear myself: I shared only a limited amount of information about my own 'story' and the reasons for my personal interest in discrimination, focusing instead on my professional experience as a PR practitioner as a means of breaking the ice. In the first two interviews, the participants were also more cautious about discussing experiences relating to race or ethnicity, or episodes of racism – perhaps because they could sense my own hesitation. However, after discussing the issue with the project steering group, I began to address race and racism more directly. As one member of the steering group pointed out, I was making race and racism the 'elephant in the room'. It was clear in the invitation what the focus of the study was, so participants would expect to be asked questions about the ways their race and/or ethnicity affected their experience. I realized that my nervousness was inadvertently reifying whiteness by silencing 'other' standpoints, and individualizing experience rather than allowing participants to connect their marginalization to broader patterns of inclusion and exclusion (Shome, 2000). Subsequently, I began the interviews with a more complete picture of my own background and experiences of difference, and this led to much more productive discussions. Participants appreciated my openness and rapport was much easier to build based on the connections we established aside from our respective professional careers. The result was a rich set of narratives that reframed PR as an industry, an occupational field and a place of work.

Structure of the book

In Chapter 2, I acknowledge the importance of history in the construction of race and racisms by situating the field of PR in the United Kingdom, its practice and its practitioners in historical context. The focus is on the ways in which different subjectivities have been attributed to people of colour, particularly colonized populations, and white British people, since these patterns form the basis of the stereotypes that have the potential to racialize BAME practitioners in PR today. I discuss the long history of BAME communities in the United Kingdom, the ways in which the British Empire constructed the 'other' in terms that confirmed the superiority of whiteness, and on the ways in which the superiority of white Britain was perpetuated within the United Kingdom after the Empire had begun to disintegrate. I consider how the PR industry was implicated in the perpetuation of Britain's domination over other countries and in the reification of whiteness, both overseas and in the domestic UK context. At the same time, I consider how histories of resistance to 'othering' among BAME communities provide an alternative, empowering narrative of identity that BAME practitioners can also draw on to counter the negative effects of racialization, as they make their way in PR.

Chapter 3 delivers an analysis of PR as an occupational field. Drawing on recent work from the sociology of occupations literature, I reflect on the parameters of PR's professionalization project and the ways in which the need to secure status and legitimacy lead the industry to construct its purpose, knowledge and practice in ways that prioritize clients and markets, but largely ignore the social and moral dimensions of PR practice. In Chapter 4, I consider how these emphases lead inevitably to the construction of a practitioner archetype that reflects a commercialized form of whiteness, an identity that aligns neatly with the environments in which PR operates, and provides evidence of PR's authority. In both chapters, I consider how the impetus to serve the needs of the occupation ultimately constructs an environment where it is easier to be white, and where BAME practitioners are always vulnerable to marginalization.

In Chapters 5 and 6, I consider the other dimension of the dialectic of diversity in PR: the voices of BAME practitioners themselves, their reflections on the field and their experiences within it. Chapter 5 deals with their critique of whiteness, the ways in which they deconstruct and challenge the apparent neutrality of the occupation towards race. In pointing out the fictional subjectivities that whiteness constructs about them and their white colleagues, they construct a heretical version of the field that has the capacity to include them on their own terms. Chapter 6 considers how their liminal understanding of the field and their position within it, allows them to manage their workplace identities and maintain some control over their careers.

Finally, in Chapter 7, I consider how a dialectical approach to analysing diversity in PR, which takes into account the impact of institutional, occupational interests on individual experience, might help us develop strategies for change. In the final analysis, I suggest that trying to improve diversity is an exercise in improving democracy in the workplace. It is much more than an economic argument; it is a moral and social imperative to which we all have the capacity to work towards.

2 Historical context

Empire, racism and public relations

Gilroy (2004) suggests that it is impossible to understand race and racism today without reflecting on the histories that have produced the conditions in which ideas of race can be perpetuated and different forms of racism can survive. The exercise creates tension because our past is part of what makes us what we are; we wish to preserve it, to hang on to its contribution, to cling to the ways of thinking that have put us in a privileged position. Yet, the 'moral and political imperative to act against the injustice of racial hierarchy' (Gilroy, 2004: 33) demands that we face up to the fact that not all of our history is good. Indeed, for the colonies that once belonged to the British Empire, it was frequently bad. Consequently, for white British academics and practitioners, what follows in this chapter is not necessarily comfortable reading.

I argue that social, political and economic dimensions of Britain's history, and the role played by PR in helping to create them, contribute to the ways in which whiteness is realized, and BAME practitioners racialized, in the PR field today. The chapter considers the historical factors that have contributed to the construction of Black and South East Asian identities in particular, both within the United Kingdom and beyond its borders. I suggest that these political, economic, social and cultural 'conditions of arrival' constitute a racialized legacy that result in particular subjectivities attributed to both white and BAME practitioners.

Locating the field and its practitioners is important because it helps to explain how and why the forms of knowledge and identity that are revealed in the empirical study are valued differently within the field, and why these valuations are so resistant to change. A 'contextual approach' (Ramamurthy, 2003: 3) offers a route to understanding the deep-rooted racialization that has shaped PR today, and revealing how PR's modern ideological clothing (re)creates the divisions of the past. It also helps to explain the origins of the power that BAME practitioners draw on to resist marginalization.

The legacy of history may not be obvious, yet it influences implicit understandings of what PR is, and who should practice it. It can make the field dysfunctional, but can also facilitate action and open up new possibilities. Its effects are complex and to a degree, unpredictable, but they are not immutable. Like the scientists who investigate DNA, once we recognize its importance to the field and its effects in different circumstances, we can interfere, take conscious measures to change what we don't like, and enhance what we do. In this sense, the history of the occupational field is the foundation for the way race is understood and incorporated into its logic today, and a source of clues as to how we might change the status quo for the better.

The chapter is organized chronologically: I begin by briefly outlining the economic, political and cultural place of Black and South-East Asian populations during the colonial period in Britain's history, before discussing the postwar environment in the United Kingdom from the 1950s onwards. The narrative illuminates the sedimented histories and subjectivities that racialized bodies carry with them into the UK PR industry today[1] by focusing on the ideological construction of 'civilizing' discourses that were (and are) dependent on definitions of the 'other' (the colonial subject, the enemy within). The categorization, regulation and normalization that 'civilization' depends on 'render specific legacies for the positioning of gender, race and class' (Skeggs, 1994: 109), legacies that BAME PR practitioners in the United Kingdom have to negotiate. In parallel with this broader historical exploration, I track the development of the PR industry from the early years of the twentieth century, exploring where links can be made between state and corporate interests, the evolution of the PR profession, and the racialized structures that mark the modern industry.

Empire, whiteness, public relations and the 'other'

Hall (2000: 217) notes 'there have always been many different ways of being "British"'; as an island nation that has been shaped by invasion and conquest, the notion that being British can be equated to whiteness is a myth, but one that has been perpetuated in history for political and economic gain. In fact, Black and Asian communities have been present in the United Kingdom for well over 500 years. Some historical records note the existence of Black soldiers in the Roman army, but certainly by the sixteenth century, Black entertainers were members of Royal courts in England and Scotland. Black people in the United Kingdom carried a reputation as a focus of spectacle, 'whose colour typecast them as devils in later drama, folklore and witchcraft' (Ramdin, 1999: 6). Blackness was also a political and ideological form of identification, rather than simply a reference to skin colour: it was perceived as evidence of impurity, cultural depravity and a lack of godliness, while whiteness represented purity and goodness (Jordan, 1969, cited in Lawrence, 1982: 58–62). The distinction has incredible longevity: more recent investigations of representations of whiteness and the 'other' tap into similar themes and oppositions (Ramamurthy, 2012; Hall, 2000; Dyer, 1997).

Britain's colonial expansion began in earnest during the eighteenth and nineteenth centuries. The British Empire was designed to drive wealth north and westwards, to London, and indigenous populations were a source of cheap or free labour that would support the profitability of colonial industries. Objectified as economic potential, they also comprised the raw material of the slave trade, from which Britain reaped enormous profits for 200 years until the abolition of the African slave trade in 1807, and the abolition of slavery in India (where approximately 16 million

Indians were enslaved) in 1841 (Ramdin, 1999). Assumptions of inferiority extended beyond bodies of colour, to the places they inhabited: indigenous environments were transformed by the British-owned sugar plantations in the Caribbean islands, by imported vegetation, and by enforced agricultural production in India, where nascent manufacturing industries were crushed in the service of British interests (Ramdin, 1999: 47). Throughout the Empire, the dominant narrative was that colonized peoples were infantile and chaotic, lacking self-control, unable to govern themselves and therefore justifiably subjected to the patriarchal control of the British government and its representatives (Ramamurthy, 2003; Ramdin, 1999; McClintock, 1995; Said, 1995).

The increasing trade between Britain and its colonies resulted in a growth in the numbers of African, Caribbean and Indian people arriving in the United Kingdom itself, either attached to the families for whom they had worked as servants, or as slaves. As a result, a community comprising African, Caribbean and Indian groups grew through the seventeenth and eighteenth centuries in London and elsewhere. Most lived in poverty, dependent on casual employment or begging, having been released by their masters but without anywhere else to go. However, some were significant figures in the higher echelons of society, prolific writers and vocal in their opposition to the slave trade and about the circumstances of the 'black poor' (Ramdin, 1999); they were an uncomfortable and visible manifestation of the treatment that the community was receiving at the hands of British society and prompted wider political and social debate about slavery and colonization.

By the end of the eighteenth century, the African and Caribbean community numbered over 10,000, was active and vibrant, and an 'integral part of the lower classes in English society' (Ramdin, 1999: 25). Indian communities also became well-established and widely dispersed during the nineteenth century, and included not only the poor, but businessmen, scholars and members of the Indian nobility (Ramdin, 1999). Despite the racist structures around them, the communities developed their own cultural identity within the British population, resisting stereotypes and retaining a sense of agency and self-determination. However, they were largely ignored in mainstream British literature and education, which was marked by cultural racism, reinforcing the intellectual and cultural inadequacy of colonized populations and sustaining the belief that whiteness, and Britain specifically, was charged with an almost God-given mission to bring civilization to the rest of the world.

PR in the United Kingdom is commonly understood to have first emerged in a formal sense in the context of the latter years of Empire, when Britain's civilizing narrative was at its height (L'Etang, 2004). During the early twentieth century, in the context of a fragmented and conflict-ridden Europe, the colonial powers of Britain, Germany and France were positioned alongside Russia as countries with the greatest influence on the region's fate. Britain had established worldwide infrastructures for trade and governance that served its political and economic interests, which needed to be preserved and, ideally, extended. Incipient forms of PR were increasingly adopted by government institutions to construct narratives that would sustain the impression of British supremacy. In other words, from its very beginnings, PR was used by the British government as an ideological tool that focused on 'national and imperial unity' (Aitken, 1990) and dominated until the 1950s (Anthony, 2012; Moloney, 2006; L'Etang, 2004).

The Empire Marketing Board (EMB), set up in 1926 and led by Sir Stephen Tallents, a major figure in the emergence of PR in the United Kingdom, was central to the development of PR's role as an indispensable element of government. The EMB was established to promote trade across the British Empire, and particularly to generate greater consumption of Empire goods in the United Kingdom. Tallents interpreted this remit in a broad, rather than specific, sense (Anthony, 2012) as an opportunity to promote an idealized narrative of the British Empire. Using a range of promotional techniques, from film and posters, to events and themed 'shopping weeks', he presented the Empire as an uncontested space where communities worked together to generate universal benefits in the form of trade and the circulation of goods and services. In so doing, he ignored the historical and current events that demonstrated exactly the opposite: resistance to British colonial rule was alive, well and growing.[2] As Aitken (1990: 94) notes, 'The intention was to construct a broad discourse of imperialist ideology, which would cement the Empire together, and challenge the growing influence of socialist ideology'.

The EMB began to emphasize partnership rather than dominance and authority, Empire as a community where political power was eclipsed by disinterested market mechanisms. At the same time, however, the Board became increasingly vocal about the unacceptability of backward social conditions in many colonies and invested in research to generate change. While its original objective was to promote trade, morality and humanitarianism intruded; the result was a promotional strategy that further reinforced the superiority of Britain's knowledge and its paternalistic role (Anthony, 2012). Constructed as a form of 'enlightened colonialism' (Coates, 2008: 217), Britain was presented as a largely benevolent world power, a hub for innovation and technology and a focus for important economic and social partnerships (L'Etang, 2004; Tallents, 1932). Its cultural superiority was also non-negotiable: Tallents, in his influential pamphlet 'The Projection of England' (1932), equated 'England' with a collection of iconic landscapes, monuments and events that referenced archetypal 'white' Britain, ignoring the contribution to English politics and culture by other long-standing ethnic minority communities.[3]

The EMB's strategy constituted a defence of Empire and Britain that did little to disturb the underlying assumption that white, western, and specifically British identities were more valuable than indigenous populations in the colonies or ethnic minority communities at home. In other words, the PR industry in the United Kingdom emerged on the back of a remit to establish the value and importance of Britain to the world (Aitken, 1990); 'others', and particularly colonized 'others', were entitled to space in the communication process only insofar as they were a potential trading partner, or represented a source of opposition that needed to be controlled. Their identities were valid if they served Britain's interests, but not on their own terms. At the same time, Tallents' modernist agenda glorified technological progress: British technologies, scientific advances, products and modern trading processes were promoted at the expense of indigenous knowledge, trade and industries, an ideological emphasis that continued during decolonization (see below). The EMB's interventions in colonial territories focused on improvements to local industry that could facilitate global trade flows, rather than stimulate local economies. The exploitation of colonial territories and populations was not questioned, and for all the recognition that social conditions were 'backward', the interests and opinions of indigenous people about their own fate remained marginalized. While the overt racism of the earlier years of Empire was not the order of the day, the ideology that characterized this period of PR's development still constructed the (classed and racialized) 'other' by omission, silencing their perspectives (Ramamurthy, 2003). Implicitly, 'other' identities were defined by the British state either as inferior, or as a potentially violent and unstable independent force that had the potential to disrupt the status quo and threaten British economic and political power. The 'other' was outside, and in opposition to, the superior British establishment.

Domestically, nation-building PR was deployed by local and national government in the first half of the twentieth century as a means of persuading the general population of the value of new state interventions in daily life. The provision of new services to local and regional populations had to be communicated to ensure take-up, and local government provided an arena where PR techniques were refined and improved by the growing number of practitioners charged with the task of enthusing voters about the new initiatives (L'Etang, 2004). The theme of national unity was promoted by national governments, who responded to the threat of fascism and totalitarianism by using propaganda to control the dissemination of ideas and manage the (unpredictable) opinions of working class men and women such that stability could be preserved. The use of propaganda became even more important during the Second World War, when films and poster campaigns encouraged the population to support the war effort (L'Etang, 2004). Public sector PR throughout this period was dominated by the need to preserve an idealized, archetypal British identity that erased conflict or dissent, and use this to counter national and international challenges to the status quo.

PR became increasingly recognized as an important tool for business from the 1920s onwards. In the context of industrialization and mass production, consumption across the Empire had to be stimulated and colonies represented markets or sources of raw materials that were legitimately exploited (Ramamurthy, 2003; Leiss *et al.*, 1997, Ewen, 1996; McClintock, 1995). At the same time, government intervention in the market – for example, by establishing state-owned monopolies – had to be guarded against. The focus of PR work in business was then very much as it is today: alongside encouraging consumption and the development of new markets, companies were advised to concern themselves with their longer-term reputation, crisis management and relationship building with important publics including government (L'Etang, 2004).

As the century progressed, the 'projection' of Britain as a unified society was difficult to sustain in an era where private industry was becoming increasingly important, and British identity was changing rapidly as a result of immigration from former colonies. Overseas, decolonization required the preservation of Britain's commercial and political dominance at the expense of 'other' interests. The PR industry's role was to reduce the risks associated with decolonization to maximize the commercial benefits it promised. Practitioners worked on behalf of the government and commercial companies to manage public opinion about Britain in newly independent states, since ensuring a peaceful transition to independence was essential to sustaining existing commercial investments and attracting new capital to former colonies. As one Unilever employee put it: 'In many of the countries where we operated, we should meet a growing spirit of nationalism, and if we met it in the wrong way, we would quickly find ourselves in the "foreign devils" class' (L'Etang, 2004: 94).

PR practitioners managed the information received by local populations about Britain and communicated positive messages about the expertise and development help that the British government and British companies could offer in their role as a 'naturally' superior sources of political, economic and scientific expertise (L'Etang, 2004: 96–97). In other words, PR implicitly reinforced the right of British corporations to continue to exploit the valuable resources that were the original prize of colonization. It supported the view that 'other' populations were in need of British development and support, and were not trusted to manage their own affairs, even after independence. Decolonization was presented as an exercise in paternalistic generosity towards still violent and unpredictable children, rather than a righting of historical wrongs; the narrative constructed by PR efforts communicated British superiority and rectitude, even in the face of rational, insistent and ultimately successful nationalist claims to self-government in its colonies. Indigenous media was dismissed as uncivilized, irrational, irresponsible or, as one PR practitioner wrote, 'wild ... editorially and technically absurd and inefficient' (L'Etang, 2004: 96). White British norms were the benchmark for judging indigenous knowledge, forms of expression and intelligence as inferior.

Thus, in the first few decades of its formal existence, PR's civilizing role was enacted at the intersection of commerce, diplomacy and national politics on a global scale, and perpetuated the colonial pattern of exploiting the natural and human resources of the global South and East for the benefit of the West and North. For all its claims to dialogue, relationship-building and two-way communication (see Chapter 3), PR's roots have a markedly undemocratic element to them, contributing to the different systems that devalued 'other' voices and frequently prevented them from being heard at all. It facilitated the way in which racism directed at colonial populations and ethnic minority communities in Britain became a form of taken-for-granted, everyday 'common-sense', 'a residual set of attitudes accumulated during the imperial period around the idea of child/savage' (Lawrence, 1982: 70). Common-sense is particularly powerful because of its normative, disciplinary effects on the daily lives of both dominant and dominated groups, and the 'condensed subjectivities' that position

BAME PR practitioners in relation to their white colleagues today, reflect in part the stereotypes that comprised the understanding of Black and Asian identities at that time.

Postwar to present day: the 1950s onwards

The necessary subjugation of the 'other', and the denigration of colonized identities in the service of Empire, left their mark on post-colonial migrant populations in the United Kingdom, whose advent in the 'mother country' prompted various manifestations of fear and consternation at both government and community level. Communities from Africa, the Caribbean and South Asia grew as a result of postwar immigration in the 1950s and 1960s, and the promise of work in a full employment labour market. However, migrants were objectified as a source of relatively cheap, manual labour, and were certainly not seen as possible candidates for skilled professional work like PR. A colour bar clearly existed in housing, employment and social life: 'No Blacks' notices in rental accommodation were common, and rents were inflated to exploit those who had little choice about where they could live (Phillips and Phillips, 1998; Ramdin, 1999). African-Caribbean groups in particular were criminalized (Hall *et al.*, 2013), while South Asian communities from India and Pakistan experienced more direct community-based racial harassment (Brah, 1992).

Communication was an important tool for managing the arrival and integration of migrant populations, but PR's origins as an occupation complicit in the protection of whiteness as a symbolically violent, universal signifier against which all other identities could be measured, also continued. Government and public sector institutions used PR to frame race as an unavoidable problem that was imposed on Britain, not of its own making. From the late 1960s onwards, and in the context of a deepening economic and social crisis, Black and Asian communities found themselves under attack from extreme right wing politicians and groups as aliens within Britain, a danger to society because of their lack of respect for authority, poor parenting, an apparent refusal to 'assimilate' (and thus acknowledge the superiority of white British identity), suspicion about their claims to British citizenship and, for black men, their predatory sexual desires towards white women (Hall *et al.*, 2013; Yuval-Davis *et al.*, 2005; Gilroy, 1987; Lawrence, 1982). Both extreme right wing and more mainstream politicians proposed deportation as a solution to the threat posed by populations whose loyalty to Britain was in doubt. Commentaries in mainstream politics and media reflected the tendency to essentialize and alienate black communities, constituting them as 'other', criminal and a destabilizing force (Hall *et al.*, 2013; Lawrence, 1982). In mainstream popular culture, racism became the raw material for stand-up comedians and even TV situation comedies; however, the humour, based on racist stereotypes, did little to dislodge 'common-sense' racism, even if the intention was to parody prejudice. Thus, the inequity that marked colonial relations was perpetuated in post-colonial times, although the systems from which it emerged differed from the imperial structures that governed the first half of the century (Hall, 2000).

Nonetheless, this period also affirmed the power of Black and Asian communities; from the 1960s onwards, they were engaged across British society, in politics, labour movements, intellectual and cultural life (Solomos, 2003; Solomos and Back, 1995). The 'race relations' industry emerged during the 1970s as part of the movement towards multiculturalism, and a good deal of public sector PR energy was directed at explaining and promoting 'equal opportunities' as an attempt to ameliorate racial tensions – although race was still presented in dualistic, essentialist terms of 'black' and 'white' rather than recognizing the increasing interpenetration of communities on each other (Hesse, 2000). At the same time, Black and Asian youth were developing their own forms of unique culture, influenced by what they saw and heard from America, their own cultural heritage and their experience as British citizens. The hybridity was expressed in music, dance and other cultural forms, epitomized in the Notting Hill Festival, which first ran in 1965, and gradually became appreciated more widely as a major cultural event (Gilroy, 1993). The desire for recognition was also reflected in the rapid expansion of ethnic media during the 1980s (Syvedain, 1993). In other words, as well as combating prejudice and racism on the streets, Black and Asian communities resisted it by asserting their own unique understanding of what it was to be British, Black and/or Asian in the 1970s and 1980s through existing political and social institutions, as well as in popular culture. Like the 'black poor' community 200 years earlier (Ramdin, 1999), their cultural and political resistance to domination challenged the constructed, exclusionary equivalence of the 'British' nation with 'white' history and culture, because it reflected the multiple historical, cultural, political and intellectual influences from beyond and within British shores, that shaped their lives and thinking as British citizens. The cultural hybridity, creativity and political agency to self-determination that characterized these complex multicultural communities (Hall, 2000) sit alongside the more negative colonial subjectivities to make up the 'sedimented histories' that accompany BAME practitioners into their workplaces today.

The PR industry expanded in the postwar period, but despite the rapidly changing social context, it remained exclusive. The industry association, the Institute of Public Relations, was set up in 1948, and the practitioners who subsequently led the professionalization of PR during the postwar years remained identified with the political, social and economic establishment: white men with impressive war records whose PR practice was grounded in networking with other elites in the media, politics and commerce (L'Etang, 2004). PR recruitment concentrated largely on people who had come into PR from the media, or who had been appointed and learnt on the job via government roles. No formal training was required to be a PR practitioner and descriptions of the 'ideal' recruit tended to rest on cultural and social capital rather than a clear skills base. Networking (often in London's private clubs, which were frequently open only to men), sociability, access to senior media contacts and the ability to understand and analyse client requirements in a broader context were all proposed as essential characteristics and reflected an unspoken class and patriarchal bias that permeated the industry (L'Etang,

2006). As part of the industry qualification developed by the Institute of Public Relations (IPR) and first run in 1956, the final exam included assessments of personality and general knowledge, rather than any formal PR skill (L'Etang, 2004). Indeed, Yaxley's (2013) oral history account of female careers during the 1970s suggests that transmitting cultural capital (e.g. knowledge about wine) and introducing young practitioners to important contacts was one common form of mentoring that the women found particularly useful. The importance of intangible skills continued into the 1980s: Bernard Ingham, the Chief Press Secretary to Prime Minister Margaret Thatcher, emphasized 'political "feel" [...], management ability [...], application, basic integrity and toughness of mind to uphold it' (Bailey and Thompson, 2012: 45). From an early stage, then, entry and progression in PR depended on cultural and social capital more easily accessed by white, male elites, but normatively understood as skills that were a 'common-sense' requirement for the occupation.

During the 1980s, Margaret Thatcher's brand of conservatism shrank public sector employment and a generation of working class communities, employed in semi-skilled and low-skilled positions, suffered greatly; minority ethnic communities were disproportionately affected because of their concentration in this kind of work. The resulting riots were popularly characterized as driven by race- and class-based divisions, particularly in the early 1980s, and Black youth were once again portrayed in the mainstream media and by politicians as dangerous, unstable and uncontrollable (Hall, 1988a: 75–79). Formal resistance came from the Black Trade Union Solidarity movement, whose members both organized and participated in industrial action (Brah, 1992). At the same time, first-generation British-born ethnic minority adults, who had moved successfully through the British education system, were countering old stereotypes of 'coloured' people as unskilled, unintelligent workers by competing for positions in white collar and professional occupations such as accounting, medicine and law, and for some, PR was an appealing career option. However, while more BAME PR practitioners joined the occupation, the inroads at this stage were small: they made up only 3 per cent of the PR workforce in the 1990s (Tyrell, 1998). Commercial PR had grown on the back of Thatcher's policy agenda during the 1980s and 1990s, and particularly as a result of the privatization of nationalized industries and deregulation of previously closed professions, but it expanded without much increase in diversity (although Bourne (2003) identified two minority-owned consultancy firms set up during this period).

Culturally, the crude racist humour of 1970s popular culture had given way by the 1990s to mainstream, complex cultural forms, created by artists from the ethnic minority communities that had originally been the butt of the joke. The TV comedy *Goodness Gracious Me*, for example, written, directed and performed by Asian actors, poked fun at the traditions of the British Asian community as well as the British environment in which they had grown up. Pop music still reflected a wide range of cultural influences; world music had become increasingly popular; and ethnic minority writers and artists became more visible and their work more widely shown (Gilroy, 2010; Hall, 1993). All this is not to say that the cultural Establishment had become open and diverse, but the 'icons' of English identity that Tallents chose for the projection of England 70 years earlier, clearly no longer provided the full picture of modern British society. This was a period of 'new ethnicities' (Hall, 1988b), where old certainties about identity and belonging started to fragment and BAME individuals became involved in a much wider cross-section of British society.

However, in 1993, Stephen Lawrence, a black British teenager, was murdered in London, a racially motivated crime that led to the publication of the Macpherson report (1999), which identified institutional racism in the police as a key factor in the failure to secure a conviction for the crime. Cultural diversity notwithstanding, British social and political institutions were forced to recognize that the naive colour blindness prompted by the neoliberal emphasis on individualism and the market had not erased racism. Following the attacks on the World Trade Centre in September 2001, the subsequent crude equation of Islam with terrorism, the wars in Iraq and Afghanistan, and the terrorist attacks in London during July 2005 (commonly known as 7/7), meant that narratives of the dangerous, uncontrollable and irrational 'other' re-emerged with a vengeance, particularly focused on Muslims, whether new migrants or long-established communities. Who and what is or isn't 'British' is once again a topic for discussion, most visibly as part of political debates on immigration and asylum that give the impression of Britain being under siege. The discussion has a gendered element, too: arranged marriage, wearing the hijab and domestic abuse within Muslim communities have all been singled out as areas where political action is required to eliminate these un-British cultural norms from UK society and ensure assimilation (Philo *et al.*, 2013; Yuval-Davis *et al.*, 2005). The 'other' has remained the cause of social instability. In response, Muslim communities in the United Kingdom have used PR to explain their position and defend themselves against prejudice, explicitly stating their allegiance to democracy, the United Kingdom and their abhorrence of terrorism (Muslim Council of Britain, 2013a, 2013b).

The legacy for BAME PR practitioners today: sedimented histories, condensed subjectivities

BAME groups now comprise a growing proportion of the middle class in Britain, with disposable income that makes them an attractive marketing target (Tyrell, 1998). Nonetheless, the disproportionately low level of BAME PR practitioners in the industry today suggests that the social and occupational histories outlined above continue to act as a source of subjectivities that accompany BAME PR practitioners and position them in relation to their peers. The identities of the 'other' constructed through the centuries of British colonial rule, and reinforced during decolonization, include associations of lower intelligence, inferior cultural and social norms, a lack of self-control, lower language and literacy skills, and an ever-present, but unpredictable, potential for challenging and disrupting the status quo. These norms were perpetuated when migrant communities became the 'enemy within' (rather than beyond) British shores and challenged the British colour bar in the 1970s and 1980s. This time, 'alien' Black bodies threatened political and social stability – as well as the very survival and purity of the nation because of the threat of miscegenation they represented. A similar rhetoric has emerged about Muslim communities since the events of 9/11. Importantly, these histories are not only about race; the economic rationale for Empire, decolonization and migration means that the systems of racialization produced through this history are also fundamentally intertwined with relations between capital and labour (Solomos *et al.*, 1982). Slaves, indentured labour and migrant communities were not only communities of colour, but also of class (Ramamurthy, 2003; Hall, 1988a). Likewise, gendered patterns of identification that operated in relation to both idealized empirical whiteness and the 'other', as well as the gendered patterns of migration and employment that marked the experience of postwar migrants (Brah, 1992), bear testimony to the importance of gender in racialization.

The history of PR in particular is a narrative of white British superiority over the 'other'. The majority of PR work in the last decades of Empire, and during decolonization, preserved the hegemonic discourse of a civilized and civilizing Britain that worked with material structures of production and consumption to marginalize the identities and interests of colonized peoples. Because of the ways in which the identities of the 'other' were constructed over time, judged as inferior to white British subjects in the areas that matter most to occupational fields (intelligence, reliability, rationality, cultural sophistication), conditions have tended to favour an assessment of white practitioners as more useful to, and more suitable for, PR. Suitability for PR was framed in terms of white, British and largely male cultural and social capital and the value attached to difference paralleled patterns in wider society. Indeed, recent research suggests UK PR practitioners still share very similar tastes and preferences, and constitute a relatively homogenous group in terms of their class and educational background (Edwards, 2008). As a consequence, BAME PR practitioners remain vulnerable to marginalization.

Corporate and government PR, which comprises the majority of PR work, continues in the same vein today, persuading the general public of the merits of neoliberal approaches to markets and governance, and participating in social networks that connect elite members of government, industry and the media in ways that protect, rather than challenge, the status quo (Leveson, 2012; Davis, 2003). The majority of PR work values the interests of white, middle class populations first and foremost,[4] and takes their identities as the normative audience for constructing and targeting communication in a way that marginalizes minority populations, including racialized, gendered and classed groups who may not represent an obvious group of consumers, voters or other valued identity (Pompper, 2013; Vardeman-Winter, 2011; Munshi and Kurian, 2005). The subordination of minority audiences by PR, exacerbated by a mainstream media environment that still relies on stereotypical, racialized interpretations of ethnic minority groups (Cottle, 2000, 1998), also contributes to the subjectivities that accompany BAME practitioners into their workplaces.

Nonetheless, BAME communities are part of mainstream British life, contributing to its modern day, multicultural form in numerous ways (Hall, 2000).

While hegemonic discourses within and outside PR can make their right to belong precarious, they can draw on a rich cultural, social and economic history to counter such challenges. The subjectivities available to BAME practitioners derive from histories of strength as well as subjugation (Yosso, 2005) and their daily lives will include positive encounters of 'multicultural conviviality' (Gilroy, 2004) where their race is not a difference that 'matters' (Werbner, 2013). In present-day terms, they also enjoy advantages in terms of their education, financial capital, middle-class status and liminal position that affords them the ability to engage and mix with a wide range of clients. They need no longer justify their position in terms of the need for 'ethnic' PR, but instead join the occupation in a wide range of roles and sectors. With a more flexible, perhaps less predictable set of subjectivities come more complex and fluid experiences. It is not a matter of course that they will be marginalized, and 'othering' may not define their careers; the value attached to their 'difference' will shift and change in the context of their occupational relations (Maynard, 1995). Their identities offer assets that they can use to negotiate their position, and indeed, they might be regarded as members of dominant rather than dominated groups, based on their class and cultural and financial capital. Both discrimination and resistance are important to the lives they live, and their narratives, discussed in Chapters 5 and 6, reveal how the balance between the two is struck from time to time and place to place.

While the history and social context set out in this chapter play a vital role in shaping experience, they do not provide the complete picture of the occupational dynamics that BAME practitioners must negotiate. Miller and Rose (1995: 428) point out that struggles over identity can only be understood if we 'address the practices that act upon human beings and human conduct in specific domains of existence, and the systems of thought that underpin these practices and are embodied within them'. History provides only one dimension of the 'systems of thought' that underpin BAME practitioners' experiences; the question remains as to what kind of occupational environment they enter, how that environment also affects the range of possibilities available to them, and the degree to which it facilitates their voice being valued as a form of agency, with the capacity to generate important changes in the field. The following chapters draw on the empirical study to deal with these questions. I begin to develop some answers in Chapter 3, introducing data that shows how PR's occupational discourses construct archetypes of practice and identity that respond to the neoliberal environment in which PR operates, and lay the foundation for an occupation unconcerned with its societal impact, characterized by a particular form of whiteness that BAME practitioners must navigate.

3 Constructing PR practice

Legitimacy, jurisdiction and the erasure of social inequity

Existing research on PR as an occupational field is minimal, and has generally focused on how occupational bodies have used structural and discursive means to demonstrate professionalism as a means of securing status (e.g. L'Etang, 2004); how practitioners use discourse to construct an occupational identity (Pieczka, 2002); and how different aspects of PR work may or may not constitute professionalism (David, 2004; Lages and Simkin, 2003). Some attention has been paid to the way that the feminization of PR has the potential to reduce its professional status or, indeed, prompts 'gender correction' (Aldoory and Toth, 2002), granting superior status to men as a means of retaining occupational status (Fitch and Third, 2010; Aldoory, 2003), and some has been paid to the territorial challenges to PR from marketing and other promotional occupations (Toledano, 2010). However, little research has engaged with the reality that PR's professional project is 'the product of a dialectical relationship with its environment' (Hanlon, 1999a: 3), is fluid and has marked exclusionary effects. While some scholars have addressed the '*hows, whens* and *whos*' (Alexander, 2006) of racism in PR, the difficult question of *why* racism happens at both institutional and interpersonal levels has not been addressed.

It is the latter perspective that I want to elaborate on in this chapter. I will not recount the arguments for or against treating PR as a formal profession; they are not relevant to the discussion I am trying to develop. Nor am I going to attempt to review the very wide field of research into occupations as it has historically evolved. Instead, my focus is on neo-Weberian analyses of occupational fields as political, competitive sites of practice (Abbott, 1988; Larson, 1977), and on recent work from the sociology of occupations that considers occupational fields as discursive arenas, where particular occupational ideologies circulate and discipline practitioners, both in terms of their practice and their self-management (e.g. Muzio and Tomlinson, 2012; Hodgson, 2002; Fournier, 1999; Grey, 1998). Both perspectives suggest occupations emerge on an ongoing basis as a result of the interaction between structures, agents, discourse and practice (Becker, 1970). They are understood as a continuous achievement, political projects engaged in the pursuit of status and power, and renewed continually in response to changes in both external and internal environments (Abbott, 1988; Larson, 1977).

A useful concept for framing the discussion in this chapter is the disciplinary logic of a field. Fournier (1999: 288) defines disciplinary logic as the 'network of accountability within which the professions have to inscribe their practice and expertise'. It is a function of the imperatives at work in the neoliberal social, political and economic environment, the criteria by which an occupation establishes its legitimacy, and the criteria by which it defines a particular set of competencies. Disciplinary logic is expressed through both habitus and discourses that define acceptable knowledge, practice and personal conduct within a field. It is a means of including some and excluding 'others', and a source of Foucauldian 'liberal government' (Fournier, 1999: 283), where the conduct of practitioners is governed at a distance through a range of techniques, including self-government. However, occupational control is never absolute: practitioners also resist injunctions to enact professions in prescribed ways.

To piece together the disciplinary logic of PR, an occupation which is always embedded within organizations, we have to begin with the historical trends in organizational development, tied to wider political and economic evolutions. Chapter 2 revealed how the origins of PR in the United Kingdom are embedded in work for, rather than resistance to, institutions that tended to perpetuate a racialized status quo, even if in the last three decades the nature of that status quo started to evolve as Black and Asian communities became more established, vocal and visible. An additional factor, vitally important for a market-oriented occupation like PR, is the shift in economic and organizational rationality over the last four decades, from bureaucratic principles of organization towards market ideals (exemplified by the best-selling *In Search of Excellence* by Peters and Waterman, 1982). The shift has moved the customer centre-stage in organizational and occupational life, and the sovereignty of the customer as the locus of institutional identity and legitimacy has superseded bureaucratic rationality, with important consequences for organizational governance. Instead of a focus on production, for example, organizations and their employees are urged to adopt a 'culture of the customer', and accommodate the demands of ever more demanding, active and innovative consumers (Du Gay and Salaman, 1992: 615). Accompanying the shift within organizations has been a fragmentation of civic spaces: 'As the language of "the market" becomes the only valid vocabulary of moral and social calculation, "civic culture" gradually becomes "consumer culture", with citizens reconceptualized as enterprising "sovereign consumers"' (Du Gay and Salaman, 1992: 622).

The neoliberal emphasis on markets, choice, consumption and organizations as drivers of wealth, has important consequences for diversity in commercial occupations like PR, which are both instrumental in the shift, and have benefited from it. PR, for example, is implicated insofar as the discourses it produces communicate the importance of the customer (broadly understood), and reflect the shift away from civic life and towards an emphasis on markets and individual choice.[1] PR has also benefited from neoliberalism because it positions itself as a unique professional service that can help organizations to understand and connect with their publics (the rapid growth of the PR industry since the 1980s, when the cult of the customer really took hold, is no coincidence).

The centrality of the customer is an important pillar in PR's corporate professionalization project. First, it is a means of legitimizing PR. As I will show later in the chapter, PR is presented as the only way to establish dialogue, rather than one-way communication, with customers (more frequently termed audiences or publics), so that a strong 'relationship' can be established with them, ultimately leading to organizational success. This logic educates PR clients that taking customers seriously is a prerequisite for their survival and makes PR – as the architect of customer relationships – indispensable. Moreover, treating all audiences as individuals with the capacity to choose, orients organizations towards using communication to identify and engage with the 'right' customers through market research and targeted communication – ultimately securing a role for PR alongside other promotional work. Finally, customer sovereignty acts as a form of disciplinary logic, in that it must be reflected in the ways that PR treats its own customers: ideally, practitioners prioritize the needs of their own clients, since client satisfaction provides the most important evidence that they are doing their job effectively, and drives both practice and revenue (Hanlon, 2004).

Customer sovereignty can only have this kind of power in the context of a society defined primarily in terms of functioning markets, where hierarchies of power that relate not to economics, but to political, social and cultural dynamics, have become less important. The latter have relevance to the disciplinary logic that governs commercial occupations only insofar as they prevent or enhance the circulation of wealth in and through markets that matter. Thus, in PR, the stage is set for the business case for diversity as a means of better engagement with particular types of customers, while the moral dimensions of power and its abuses are of little consequence for commercial success. In an occupation so tightly connected to commerce and neoliberal agendas, inequity is not simply masked, but is practically erased from the field's discourses about its legitimacy and jurisdiction. As a result, important experiences of marginalization in the occupational field go unspoken, even if they have the potential to affect the quality of PR work, because there is no acceptable language in which to express them. There are simply very few words within neoliberal discourse that make sense of a moral, historical and socio-cultural starting point for tackling diversity (Couldry, 2010). Bias, discrimination, racism, prejudice – all are concerns that address morality rather than markets, and therefore have no obvious place in PR's journey towards legitimacy.

The erasure of moral discourse means that diversity cannot be discussed as a locus of inequity, but only as a form of individual or organizational market advantage. Things begin and end with the market; this, as Noon (2007) has pointed out, leaves diversity initiatives vulnerable as market pressures evolve, since if the market does not require diversity, it may be put aside as a concern. Moreover, a market-based rationale for PR has the potential to legitimize continued inequity: if businesses decide diversity can be 'outsourced' more cheaply (for example, by employing an 'ethnic communications' company rather than employing more diverse people on their own staff), or that diversity might cause more problems than benefits, it becomes a casualty of cost and efficiency concerns (Noon, 2007;

Carbado and Gulati, 2003). It also makes suspect those who advocate for a wider interpretation of the importance of diversity, since they introduce what Bourdieu (1991: 129) has called 'heretical discourse' – language that undermines the legitimate discourses of the rest of the field. Fear of heresy acts to silence marginalized practitioners who wish to enjoy a successful career in the field. Racialization in PR, then, begins with the erasure of marginal voices and the negation of their perspectives.

In the next section, I discuss in more detail the framework I adopt for understanding PR as an occupational field. The discussion forms the theoretical groundwork for the second half of the chapter, an empirical analysis of the identity constructed through PR's occupational discourses. The chapter concludes with a reflection on how normative understandings of what PR is and does in the world, mask the racialization of the field, and ultimately create the conditions through which BAME practitioners can be marginalized as 'outsiders-within'.

Knowledge-based occupations and corporate professionalization

PR can be defined as a knowledge-intensive occupation, one of a number of occupations which differ from traditional professions in that they have a fluid body of occupational knowledge, few barriers to entry, optional professional training and are inseparable from organizations in practice (Kipping *et al.*, 2006). Examples include management consultancy, project management and recruitment (Muzio *et al.*, 2011). PR's knowledge base is broad rather than specific, no specific degree is required for entry into the profession, industry bodies offer certified training courses but they are not compulsory, and there is no formal career path of the kind found in law, medicine, accounting or engineering, although job titles do correspond to a certain stage in peoples' careers (e.g. account executive, account manager, communications director). PR services are usually designed to be implemented on behalf of organizations, so that client needs and demands are fundamental to the occupation's survival.

Knowledge-intensive occupations are 'ambiguous domains, in which expertise can no longer be isolated from other experts, decision makers or clients' (Noordegraaf, 2007: 780). In their efforts to legitimize their existence, they engage in 'corporate professionalization projects', responding to occupational and organizational imperatives in different ways depending on the demands of the situation (Muzio and Kirkpatrick, 2011; Noordegraaf, 2007). Like other occupations, they use the resources available to them (individuals with specific skill sets and forms of capital, networks of clients and market demand) to associate prestige with their activities and maintain a market for their services, often drawing on characteristics associated with traditional professions (Larson, 1977). PR's corporate professionalization project, for example, has included making claims to deliver a public service, historically associated with traditional professions such as law and medicine. In the process, occupations use both discourse and practice to lay claim to a specific body of knowledge and expertise that allows them to be identified as a legitimate field of activity (Hodgson, 2002). For occupations that have a weak foundation in material outputs, the use of discourse as a means of constructing and justifying their existence is particularly important (Alvesson, 1994: 544).

PR's claims to legitimacy should be understood, therefore, as a competitive strategy, designed to preserve and improve its status in a world where its right to exist must constantly be justified (Abbott, 1988). At the same time, they constitute a set of 'truths' on which the occupation's ability to govern practitioners depends (Fournier, 1999; Miller and Rose, 1990). Convincing statements about why PR is required, what it is and how it can resolve particular problems, both establish its superiority as a promotional occupation, and are essential to the willingness of practitioners to 'buy into' the disciplinary logic of the field.

Constructions of professional knowledge that define the professional project are also linked to archetypal practitioner identities, which draw on knowledge, experience and personal attributes such as gender, race and class, and on subjective criteria including 'professionalism', personality or embodiment (Sommerlad, 2008b; Bolton and Muzio, 2007). As noted in Chapter 2, historically, PR has delimited entry to those who demonstrated an appropriate racial and class background and (frequently) a public service career history (L'Etang, 2004). Such strategies are typical of the ways that professional projects establish status hierarchies within their fields that tend to reinforce existing social divisions. Indeed, Anthias (2013) points out that discrimination by race, class or gender, while frequently presented as a materially grounded categorization with concrete rationales (e.g. that marginalized individuals are less skilled, or less well-educated), is in essence a discursive, disciplinary exercise in power, an argument that points to the importance of paying attention to how discourse itself communicates occupational hierarchies. From this perspective, corporate professionalization projects are best understood as inherently political, ideologically driven, collective efforts to achieve social mobility by controlling an occupation's internal structures, practitioner behaviour, and external reputation through discourses and practices that reflect, rather than challenge, broader patterns of social inequity (Bolton and Muzio, 2008; Larson, 1977; Johnson, 1972). In Witz's succinct opinion (1992), they are political projects of closure.

Occupational habitus and diversity

Corporate professionalization projects are reflected in the doxa of the field, the rules of the occupational 'game' that practitioners follow instinctively and reproduce as the occupational habitus. Doxic discourses set out the rationale and purpose of an occupation and expectations of its practitioners (Gunnarsson, 2009), providing a field-wide ideological framework within which the right to occupational membership can be assessed. The main architects of the doxa are the occupational elite, including professional associations (e.g. in PR, the CIPR and PRCA), who have the symbolic authority to speak and act 'on behalf of' the occupation (Bourdieu, 1991), as well as organizations or individuals generally regarded as 'successful' in the context of the field (e.g. the elite global PR firms such as Hill & Knowlton, Edelman, Ketchum Pleon, Weber Shandwick). The latter have status in their own right as global institutions providing employment and disseminating practice, but are also frequently closely involved with the operation of professional associations and therefore have multiple spheres of influence (Flood, 2011; Muzio *et al.*, 2011).

Within the logic of the doxa, certain practices, particular forms of behaviour and embodiment, including modes of dress, speech and interaction, become normalized as the occupational habitus. They demonstrate an ability to fit in with the occupational archetype, serve occupational interests and communicate professionalism to clients (Anderson-Gough *et al.*, 2006; Grey, 1998; Alvesson, 1994). To draw on the theatrical metaphor used by Becker *et al.* (2009 [1961]: 4), PR's habitus communicates the part that practitioners must play in the 'drama' of public relations. As Bourdieu (2000: 100) argues, demonstrating the potential to embody the appropriate habitus and play the right part is a requirement for new entrants to any field:

> In reality, what the new entrant must bring to the game is not the habitus that is tacitly and explicitly demanded there, but a habitus that is practically compatible, or sufficiently close, and above all, malleable and capable of being converted into the required habitus, in short congruent and docile, amenable to restructuring. That is why operations of co-option [...] are so attentive not only to the signs of competence, but also to the barely perceptible indices, generally corporeal ones – dress, bearing, manners – of dispositions to be, and above all, to become, one of us.

Bourdieu's attention to signs and indices is particularly important because it calls out the importance of embodiment as the basis for implicit judgements about occupational suitability that may not be completely under an individual's control. In other words, it is not enough just to 'learn the lines'; an appropriate 'performance' of PR is as much visceral as it is verbal and cognitive (Becker *et al.*, 2009 [1961]). How people perceive us when we walk into an interview room can only be managed to a certain extent: we cannot hide our ethnicity or gender, and embodied elements of habitus such as different forms of language, accent and comportment are difficult to adjust convincingly (Bourdieu, 1991).

Our bodies are ineradicable vessels for the subjectivities that others attribute to us (Gilroy, 2004); Bourdieu's contribution makes clear that these subjectivities will be important to the stratification of PR, a source of racialization in the working lives of BAME practitioners, and the basis of their responses to such effects. Plenty of research has shown how racialized and gendered identities, that do not seem to fit an occupational habitus, become vulnerable to marginalization (Sommerlad, 2009). In the UK accounting profession, for example, ethnic minority practitioners face overt and covert barriers to entry and curtailed career advancement (Kyriacou and Johnston, 2011; Weisenfeld and Robinson-Backmon, 2007; Ram and Carter, 2003). In South Africa, exclusion from informal interactions, stereotyping and pressure to conform to a white British professional habitus all mark the experiences of Black South African accountants in the post-apartheid era (Hammond *et al.*, 2012). Studies by Mirza (2006) and Ahmed (2007b) on diversity and the experience of Black women in the academy illustrate how their bodies are visible as institutional tools for demonstrating diversity, but that this is often the limit of engagement between these white institutions and their 'other' employees. Ethnic minority academics' skills were questioned, they were assumed to specialize in research related to ethnicity, they were perceived as less authoritative than male colleagues, and they had to negotiate environments where whiteness was institutionalized and their voices were largely silenced (Bagilhole and Goode, 2001). Other research has noted the challenges that ethnic minority women face in managing very different expectations in their work and home lives, including cultural and religious requirements (such as fasting or praying) that have to be accommodated alongside existing responsibilities (Kamenou, 2008). In law, journalism and accounting, a gendered habitus has led to women being excluded from networking, subjected to sexist treatment, having to negotiate long working hours, and generally being perceived as less capable, less skilled and less authoritative than their male colleagues (North, 2009; Anderson-Gough *et al.*, 2005; Claringbould *et al.*, 2004; Sommerlad, 2002; Kay and Hagan, 1998; Thornton, 1996).

In PR, research has confirmed similar patterns of exclusion for women, and has also shown how raced and gendered identities have shaped the working lives of practitioners. Women continue to occupy less senior positions than men, are paid less than men and must navigate organizational expectations derived in part from wider gender-based norms in society (PR Week, 2013a; Daymon and Demetrious, 2010; Fitch and Third, 2010; Toth and Cline, 2007). Early studies of African American female practitioners' experiences in PR found that, while they occupied middle management roles and found their work fulfilling (Kern-Foxworth *et al.*, 1994), they were paid less than their white counterparts, and their salaries did not reflect their seniority (Kern-Foxworth, 1989). They still commonly experience implicit or explicit racism, stereotyping and pigeonholing (Gallicano, 2013; Ford and Appelbaum, 2009; Tindall, 2009, 2007; Pompper, 2004; Len-Rios, 1998; Zerbinos and Clanton, 1993). Pompper (2005) has highlighted the processes by which White behaviour, understandings, norms and expectations are instilled through PR research and practice that presents alternative views of the world as 'different', non-standard and judged in light of their separateness.

Taken as a whole, the body of work on the experiences of women and ethnic minority groups in occupational fields demonstrates that fields demand 'docility and passivity' from 'outsiders-within' (Hill-Collins, 1990). The need is for a 'mythic, holistic "good Other"', not too potent or different or indeed authentic so as to pose a real threat to other individuals or to a socially cohesive society' or, in this context, a socially cohesive occupation (Malik, 2013: 231). The need for acquiescence to the norm is communicated to ethnic minority practitioners not only by implicit or explicit sanctions (such as slower career progress, or disciplinary issues), but also through informal and formal occupational discourses that help to communicate the ways in which conformity should be enacted. How an occupation is described and justified simultaneously communicates what a practitioner should 'be' if they want to fit in. As the rest of the chapter shows, and in line with the customer- and market-centric disciplinary logic, the imperative in PR is to be someone who can perform an appropriately commercial (and commercially viable) identity.

Communicating habitus through discourse

As an ideological social practice, discourse is an important channel through which some identities and practices are privileged by the occupational habitus and others disadvantaged (Fairclough, 2003; Mumby and Stohl, 1991). Evaluations of difference, in terms of who does and does not conform to occupational norms in practice, knowledge or conduct, are a fundamental structuring principle of occupational discourses, that 'organize occupational identity and reproduce occupational segregation' (Ashcraft, 2007: 28). From a Foucauldian perspective, occupational discourse articulates the links between occupational knowledge, conduct and identity that discipline practitioners into the ways of the occupational field (Hodgson, 2003; Fournier, 1999). As Alvesson (1994: 540) notes, it is contextualized by the habitus, which frames the ways in which 'talk is competently used for specific purposes in "cultural action"', guiding the enactment of occupations 'on the ground' by their practitioners with a set of norms to which they are supposed to adhere (Hodgson, 2003). It is not only occupational discourses that exercise such power: Acker (2006) points out the importance of disciplinary discourses and habitus in organizations, which exercise direct control (formal, process and practice) and indirect control (informal, internalized by employees) over their members to sustain existing hierarchies. Practitioners in PR, whose practice is inseparable from the organizations that buy their services, will therefore be subject to disciplinary discourses from both occupation and organization, which will interact to govern their behaviour and define their occupational and organizational status.

Occupational discourses communicate ideological abstractions, rather than representations of reality, that serve the purpose of presenting the occupation in ways that support its struggles for legitimacy. They may be generalizations, but they are important because '[p]ublic jurisdiction concerns an abstract space of work, in which there exist clear boundaries between homogeneous groups. Differences of public jurisdiction are differences between archetypes' (Abbott, 1998: 60). In other words, occupational discourse communicates occupational archetypes that can be used to differentiate an occupation from its competitors and link its work to sources of legitimacy. They are enacted normatively through 'modes of rhetoric' (Grey, 1998: 571); they communicate occupational function and knowledge – what might be practiced – and occupational identity – who may practice and how they may practice (Evetts, 2011; Ashcraft, 2007; Cohen *et al.*, 2005; Aldridge and Evetts, 2003; Anderson-Gough *et al.*, 1998).

Occupational discourses are complex and multiple; they overlap, reinforce and sometimes contradict each other. They address both practice and identity;

the two areas are linked, of course, and are often addressed simultaneously in texts, so that their effects are mutually dependent. Analytically, however, it is helpful to separate them so that processes of exclusion can be more clearly understood. The focus in the remainder of this chapter is on discourses that relate to practice and clarify what PR 'is' in today's world. The aim is to explore how they contribute to PR's corporate professionalization project, its struggle to maintain legitimacy and jurisdiction. In the process, I demonstrate how they structure an occupational habitus that both disconnects PR from the wider social, cultural and political context by focusing almost exclusively on PR's contribution to organizational well-being and success, and masks the racializing effects it has on practitioners' lives by erasing inequity from the set of legitimate concerns for the field.

It should be clear from the above discussion that my analytical starting point is that the discourses are not designed to reflect the reality of day-to-day practice, but rather serve as a means of representing the occupation in a particular way, so that PR's jurisdiction may be established and maintained. Moreover, the discourses are relational in the sense that corporate professionalization projects are enacted in a competitive context; survival is ensured by controlling tasks and jurisdiction in relation to competition from other occupations, or to institutions on whom occupational legitimacy depends, including government, legislature, academia, the media, clients and competing occupations (Fournier, 1999; Abbott, 1988). The relational nature of discourse may or may not be explicit – the CIPR may say how PR differs from marketing, or may choose not to mention marketing at all when defining PR, for example. Regardless, the discourses should be read as disciplinary mechanisms that shape practice and identity in ways that respond to existing or future occupational challenges.

A final caveat is in order. Discourses are always contested, and those presented below are no exception. My argument is not that the world of PR they construct is definitive and absolute, but that it is normative. In other words, the discourses exert a certain power over those subjected to it, to conform to its imperatives as the way things are, or should be. However, norms are frequently contested and, as Foucault's work has shown, power can produce agency as well as subjugate it. In Chapters 5 and 6 I illustrate how BAME PR practitioners challenge the archetypes that are set out below.

A note on method

The empirical study on which the book is based draws was a multi-method investigation of the experiences of BAME PR practitioners in the United Kingdom, funded by the UK's Economic and Social Research Council (ESRC).[2] The aim was to establish the occupational context for their experiences, to understand their narratives of what it is like to be an minority ethnic practitioner in PR today, and to connect these insights together in order to build a picture of how race and racialization shapes the occupation.

The material in this chapter is based on a critical discourse analysis of industry texts that described the occupation and its practitioners. These texts were examples of the occupational discourse produced by the two industry associations, the CIPR and the PRCA, and the leading (largest and most profitable) consultancies in the field, organizations that enjoy symbolic authority within the field and therefore have a powerful normative influence on PR practitioners and the work they do. The texts were:

- Web pages from the CIPR ad PRCA websites that described the profession and its practitioners.
- Downloadable PDF documents from the CIPR and PRCA websites that described PR, its purpose and value, and provided advice about how to enter and progress in the industry.
- Websites of the top 10 consultancies in the *PRWeek* Top 150 2009 (PR Week, 2009): Hill & Knowlton, Weber Shandwick, Edelman, Freud Communications, Fishburn Hedges, Brunswick, Finsbury, Financial Dynamics, Citigate Dewe Rogerson and Chime Communications.

The industry association websites (accessed December 2010 and again in December 2011) describe the role and importance of PR in organizations and wider society, disseminate research and information to practitioners, clients and prospective entrants, and provide training and resources for members. For the analysis, I chose pages that described the role and function of PR and the skills and attributes necessary to enter and succeed in a career as a PR practitioner. In other words, these were the pages that constructed an archetypal identity and purpose for the occupation and its practitioners. In Abbott's (1988) terms, they articulated the basis for the occupation's legitimacy and jurisdiction in the public and workplace arenas.

Consultancy websites (accessed January 2010) are designed specifically to persuade current and potential clients of the merits of PR as delivered by that particular organization, and reflect organizational habitus as well as wider occupational norms. All consultancy sites had a similar basic structure, with three main sections: descriptions of the consultancy's jurisdiction and company ethos, frequently designated as 'Who we are', or 'About us'; descriptions of the consultancy's approach to work and specialist areas of practice ('What we do'); and evidence of expertise in the form of cases or client testimonials ('Our clients'). Some included profiles of practitioners and a relatively brief section on 'Careers' for prospective employees. The focus was the web texts rather than visuals, since these contained the most detailed articulation of PR's identity and purpose. However, practitioner images were incorporated into the analysis where they appeared, given that they provided a visual interpretation of occupational identity in relation to the text.

Both sources of data can be understood as promotional texts that represent (ontologically define), advocate (legitimize and justify) and anticipate (prompt action) on behalf of the subject of the text (Wernick, 1991). For example, the CIPR home page (CIPR, 2013a) argues that 'public relations not only tells an organization's story to its publics, it also helps to shape the organization and the way it works' and that '[e]ffective PR can help manage reputation by communicating and building

(Continued)

(Continued)

good relationships with all organization stakeholders'. Implicit in the selected texts, therefore, is a legitimating function exercised on behalf of PR as an occupation and consultancies as organizations delivering PR expertise. Following Fairclough (2003), the texts are also understood as social events produced in, and producing, interaction between different social actors (practitioners, consultant organizations, new entrants, industry associations and potential and existing clients).

The normative world of PR: communicative societies and the value of reputation

The logic that PR draws on invokes the wider political and economic context: the market, the sovereign consumer, the reification of technology and the networked society, and the sovereignty of the client (organization and individual) (Fournier, 1999; Du Gay and Salaman, 1992). Public relations cannot lay claim to a clear, scientific body of knowledge because it deals with the production and effects of communication, both largely unquantifiable processes that are hard to pin down in terms of predictable sequences of events or activities. This puts it at a significant disadvantage as compared with marketing or advertising, where measuring the effects of communication is much easier. Instead, PR discourses deflect attention away from prediction and measurement, and ground jurisdictional claims in an interpretation of reality that emphasizes chaos and unpredictability, where PR, as a strategic yet flexible tool, is indispensable. In so doing, they draw on existing narratives of postmodern, complex societies to legitimize the existence of PR in an inherently communicative, fragmented, yet networked world (Castells, 2000; Lash and Urry, 1994). Rapid economic, social and political change, increased uncertainty, competition on a global scale, and ever new forms of connectivity mean the ability of organizations to control their destiny is a thing of the past. Instead, reputational and commercial risks abound as a result of stakeholders, influencers and audiences freely exchanging opinions and information about an organization.

> The climate in which companies operate has shifted seismically and corporate reputation has never been so vulnerable. Business today is subject to ever increasing scrutiny from a complex set of stakeholders and influencers whose opinions can create more impact than ever before.
>
> (Edelman, 2010)

Such a fluid environment cannot be fully controlled; risk is ever-present. Nonetheless, in a communicative society, conversations about organizations do not, per se, threaten organizational objectives. Rather, the concern is with conversations that could damage reputation, since a loss of reputation can lead to increased scrutiny and imposed (rather than voluntary) changes in practice. Here, there is scope for organizations to shape their destiny by using PR to exert control over their relationships with audiences. With no intervention from PR, organizations and their audiences exist in opposition to each other; audiences are a potential threat, because they 'scrutinize' organizational activity. Scrutiny suggests a focus on detail, shedding light on areas previously hidden, and an authority on the part of those who scrutinize to challenge the choices that organizations make about their daily business. But with PR, organizations can win over sceptical audiences through listening, conversation and dialogue, respond to them, and thereby better protect the organization's reputation.

> Digital and social media channels have transformed today's communications landscape. Conversations about brands and services are happening every day. We help brands to earn the right to be a part of these conversations and become catalysts for new conversations.
>
> (Fishburn Hedges, 2010a)

In other words, an organization must partner with the 'sovereign consumer' (Du Gay and Salaman, 1992: 616) who would scrutinize it, in order to 'drive the agenda' (Edelman, 2010) that will govern their thoughts and discussions from a distance. This logic allows PR's fundamental value to organizations to be defined in terms of reputation, a universal cure-all that leads to understanding, support and desirable behaviour from the all-important customer:

> Public relations is the discipline which looks after reputation, with the aim of earning understanding and support and influencing opinion and behaviour. It is the planned and sustained effort to establish and maintain goodwill and mutual understanding between an organisation and its publics.
>
> (CIPR, 2009a)

Making reputation the locus of PR work has significant advantages, given that its jurisdiction can never be permanently settled because the occupational environment is constantly in flux (Hodgson, 2007: 39; Abbott, 1988). Advances in knowledge and technology, for example, result in competition over territory and redefinition of tasks that challenge the social dimension of PR's jurisdictional control (external to the field), while changing social norms may produce shifts in occupational roles and responsibilities that challenge the cultural dimension (internal to the field) (Abbott, 1988). These challenges must be managed to repel the threat of encroachment by related occupations (Hutton, 2010). Using sales, promotion, publicity or even media relations to describe what PR 'is' would fail to establish jurisdictional boundaries, since marketers, events managers, journalists, citizen journalists and advertisers all engage with the same areas. Reputation, on the other hand, is complex, intangible, always under threat in a fast-changing environment, and sets PR apart from its competitors. The implicit claim is that marketers and advertisers cannot address reputation because they are ultimately engaged in selling and promoting, and the latter constitute one-way communication rather than dialogue. Only PR can help organizations 'earn' support, a phrase which suggests a deeper, more genuine engagement with audiences and an understanding of both sides of debates that constitute a reputational threat.

Constructing expertise: PR's 'body of knowledge'

Framing PR in terms of the complexities of reputation also helps shifts the focus away from the reality that PR is actually based on the universally available, intangible skill of 'communication', and instead allows the field to allude to a body of objective, identifiable and exclusive expertise, a set of 'specialized truths and rare powers' (Miller and Rose, 1990: 2) that are crucial to legitimacy. Indeed, some kind of claim to specialist knowledge is essential to professional status, since it is a means of distinguishing both practice and practitioner from other occupations (Friedson, 2001; Abbott, 1988; Larson, 1977; Johnson, 1972). As well as supporting claims to professionalism, specialist knowledge allows an occupation to maintain exclusivity over certain tasks, and task control, as Abbott (1988) points out, is an central organizing principle of professional projects.

While claiming a scientific body of knowledge is unsustainable given the difficulty PR faces in clearly measuring and validating its effects (Watson and Noble, 2007), nonetheless the texts imply an exclusive and sophisticated normative form of epistemological authority for the occupation (Friedson, 2001), as a means of shoring up PR's claims to professional status. Reputation positions PR work far from a 'buy/sell' engagement with audiences; it involves creating understanding, an essential success criteria (we have already been informed) for operating in a highly complex environment. While PR's exclusive knowledge base may not be scientific in the traditional sense, the language used to describe the occupation echoes the higher-status, more 'scientific' bodies of knowledge that are claimed by traditional professions such as medicine. The CIPR definition above, for example, uses the pseudo-scientific language of 'discipline', planning and 'publics' (all of which appear in widely used academic definitions of PR) and suggests a strategic, rather than tactical, function. It emphasizes the planned, long-term nature of PR's 'effort' (this work is not easy, after all). PR, then, requires thought, vision and 'discipline' (in order to be a 'discipline' and to 'discipline' audiences), suggesting a body of knowledge that is complex, abstract and can only be applied by experts. The claim to professionalism implicit in presentations of PR expertise is reinforced by PR's status as a graduate occupation, confirming that only people with high levels of intelligence can carry out the job: 'the most important thing [to enter the field] is to have a good degree and an excellent academic record' (PRCA, 2009).

Alvesson (1994), in his study of advertising agents, notes that the construction of distance between client capability and consultant expertise is important for occupational credibility, underpinning the impression that the service really has something unique to offer. PR is constructed in the texts as a form of expertise, a set of 'disinterested truths' (Miller and Rose, 1990: 10) that are brought in to the organization as a means of navigating the environment, managing challenges that prevent it from achieving its objectives, and helping it to achieve broader goals. It doesn't matter what kind of organization is in need; reputation, as the promised result of PR work, is relevant to all organizations, all over the world. Case studies and client testimonials are used to illustrate the success that a PR intervention can deliver in any circumstance. Indeed, the growth and ubiquity of the occupation, emphasized by the industry associations, provides evidence that it is a valued source of objective insight into communications issues in a diverse range of contexts.

> Public relations can play a critical role in achieving competitive advantage by, for example, opening new markets, attracting high-calibre employees, giving more access to funding and investors, creating a high value for products and services, and protecting business in times of crisis.

> (PRCA, 2011)

The advantage of claiming knowledge that has no limits to its application is significant because it allows PR to grow rapidly and practitioners to claim a universally applicable set of skills. However, at the same time, claims to universality contain the seeds of PR's own fallibility. While believing in reputation as a cure-all fits neatly within a neoliberal economic and political framework focused on the importance of market mechanisms over government intervention, the sovereign consumer, and organizations as active agents for the distribution of wealth (Harvey, 2005; Du Gay and Salaman, 1992), market-based conceptions of reputation oriented solely towards audiences-as-customers have limitations that mean, in practice, unquestioning belief in its power to solve all problems may be difficult to sustain.

The limitations begin with the way PR defines the environment in communicative terms and focuses on reputation as a solution for the risk and potential conflict that organizations may face. This generates a narrow understanding of society and the audiences that may be relevant to PR work. Conceptualizing 'publics' in terms of their communication behaviour does not require PR practitioners to recognize the multiple sources of privilege and disadvantage that shape audience attitudes and prompt action. More important is whether they are talking about organizations in uncontrolled channels, expressing uncontrolled views, or indeed, whether they are audiences that organizations would like to be talking about them, buying their products or supporting their cause. Material forms of disadvantage, such as the inequitable overall distribution of power and wealth, or racial discrimination, are less visible in a world viewed through the lens of connectivity, mobility and 'conversations'. Indeed, more often than not, those who suffer from material disadvantage are not the publics that commercial or government organizations want to converse with: fewer of them vote, they have less to spend, and the 'market' they represent may be relatively small.

Failing to recognize that social inequality influences behaviour towards organizations means the occupation is poorly equipped to address some of the biggest threats their clients face, given that the frustrations borne of social inequality are a significant source of risk to organizations (O'Brien *et al.*, 2000). There are ample examples: the regular demonstrations at G20 and G8 meetings, the Occupy movement, and, closer to home for UK PR, the 2009 riots in the City of London, when financial institutions faced angry crowds of demonstrators intent on inflicting material damage on buildings and business, as well as the riots during summer 2012 in a number of UK cities, where businesses small and large were the focus of disenfranchised groups' anger. Regardless of the claim that PR will protect organizational reputation by communicating well, it cannot change the reality that organizations, institutions and elite individuals enjoy privileges that sustain the systemic inequities people are subjected to as a result of their race, class, gender, sexuality or other identity. These are not 'communication problems' (Windahl and Signitzer, 1992), but relate to bigger material issues; 'goodwill and understanding' between organizations and publics is much more difficult to achieve once they are taken into account.

The fact that complex social inequalities are 'airbrushed' out of the organizational landscape presented in PR discourses makes sense in terms of PR's professional project and disciplinary logic. After all, occupational discourse is an ideological, promotional tool. Raising doubts about PR's claims to universal effectiveness makes no sense; leaving them out deflects attention away from potential challenges to PR's legitimacy, and sustains the focus on communicative dynamics, where legitimacy can be more easily substantiated through case studies and client endorsements. From this perspective, the erasure of inequity is necessary for the survival of the occupation.

Conclusion: the erasure of inequity

The focus on communicative societies, organizations, and reputation that defines PR's doxa delivers a coherent and relatively clear basis for PR to argue its jurisdiction as a source of risk management for organizations in a complex world. As a knowledge-intensive occupation, PR discourses would be expected to balance occupational and organizational interests, but in fact the neoliberal environment means that it is relatively easy for a largely commercial occupation like PR to construct its occupational interests in terms of organizational interests, markets and customers. The overwhelming impression from the documents is that PR is mainly implemented for organizations, and the abstract, objective and specialist knowledge that defines the field accrues value based on its ability to improve organizational fortunes in the face of challenges from potentially difficult audiences. As in other corporate professionalization projects, 'truth' has to be expressed in terms that correspond to the organizations in which practitioners work, must differ from the expertise provided by competitive occupations, and must be acceptable to other sources of occupational legitimacy such as legislative bodies or the media (Fournier, 1999). PR discourses realize these three imperatives by drawing on the language of management, strategy, consumerism and the market, to claim a valuable place in society alongside other professional groups.

PR' s legitimacy is reinforced by explicit claims that it provides some form of societal benefit in ways disconnected from the organizations for which it works, a common strategy for occupations struggling to defend their territory in the public arena (Abbott, 1988). It is particularly important for PR to make such claims, since its struggle for legitimacy frequently plays out in moral terms. The occupation faces continuous attacks on the ethics of its practices and practitioners in light of its increasing influence on political, economic and social debates (Leveson, 2012; Lewis *et al.*, 2008; Miller and Dinan, 2008). In response, the CIPR has adopted a two-pronged strategy based on claims to traits associated with traditional professionalism: a robust professional ethics and serving the public interest, on the one hand, and the mastery of technical skills derived from a 'scientific' body of knowledge, on the other (Pieczka, 2007). However, the umbilical cord that links PR to organizations remains even here. The PRCA and CIPR codes of practice (CIPR, 2013b; PRCA, 2013c) stipulate in general terms that practitioners should carry out their work with regard for the public interest, but specifics relate to professionalism within the context of the client relationship, rather than the public good.

Nonetheless, on the websites, organizational benefit is framed in societal terms. The main focus is on talking with audiences, rather than at them. Organizations that use PR are implicitly constructed as benevolent partners, able to protect the public interest while serving their own purposes (the reality that these may be diametrically opposed is ignored). Indeed, the texts imply that PR practitioners must be concerned with the public interest, if they are to carry out their organizational role effectively.

> 'Understanding' is a two-way process. To be effective, an organisation needs to listen to the opinions of those with whom it deals and not solely provide information. Issuing a barrage of propaganda is not enough in today's open society.
>
> [...]
>
> At its best, public relations not only tells an organisation's story to its publics, it also helps to shape the organisation and the way it works. Through research, feedback communication and evaluation, the practitioner needs to find out the concerns and expectations of a company's publics and explain them to its management.
>
> (CIPR, 2011b)

Consultancy discourses locate value firmly within the parameters of organizational work (connecting with audiences, engaging with opinion formers, making the most of communication networks), but in a neoliberal environment, this too can be argued as a form of societal benefit, since organizations that achieve their goals presumably make money and provide employment that would otherwise be lost. PR in the public interest, then, rests on two-way communication, avoiding 'propaganda', acting as an agent of change and a channel through which an organization can listen to its stakeholders, thereby giving the public a voice in organizational matters and developing mutual understanding. The implicit claim is that PR is a mechanism through which organizational and public interests might be balanced for the greater good – perhaps even protecting against the abuse of organizational power in society. But it is hard to be convinced by such arguments, given the overwhelming emphasis on PR's organizational remit elsewhere in the discourses and the regularity of public challenges to PR ethics. The default justification for PR's legitimacy is organization-centric: its jurisdiction is located within organizations; the argument for valuing organizational engagement in dialogue with audiences is only ever articulated in relation to organizational objectives.

In summary, constructing PR's role and value in terms of organizational reputation ensures that clients recognize its legitimacy, but simultaneously contains expectations of its impact to the organizational domain while dismissing the reality that PR might have a wider impact. In line with the disciplinary logic of the field, it echoes the neoliberal primacy of markets, customers and choice, and the erasure of civic identities and priorities (Couldry, 2010; Du Gay and Salaman, 1992). PR is not understood as a powerful locus of social, political or cultural meaning that shapes society; it shapes organizations' fortunes. The cumulative effect of individual PR campaigns as a source of sustained discrimination or, alternatively, societal change, is largely ignored. Even in the industry associations' codes of practice, the possibility that PR and its practitioners might be able to work with reference to wider societal, cultural or political concerns is left out of the picture. Inequity, or its alleviation, is neither part of the normative context for PR, nor a possible outcome of PR work – although it may, of course, underpin the objectives of third sector organizations using PR.

The doxic emphasis on organizations also constrains professional reflexivity and prompts an ahistorical understanding of society and PR itself. At an occupational level, it removes the need to recognize the historical conditions that have given rise to the occupation. As Chapter 2 illustrated, the latter are soaked in race and class divisions that produced and maintained inequity both within and outside the occupational field. Making this explicit could start useful conversations about whether and how some practitioners are more marginalized than others in the occupation; ignoring it makes finding a starting point for such discussions (other than simply pointing out numerical imbalances) more difficult. Unfortunately, the relative power enjoyed by the white, middle- and upper-class groups in British society, from which the majority of PR practitioners benefit (as opposed to the organizational power they enhance) is not relevant to the corporate professionalization project and can therefore be put to one side – if indeed it is actively considered at all.

Racialization in PR, then, begins with the ways the occupation constructs its jurisdiction and argues its legitimacy, via an occupational doxa that produces a habitus where forms of discrimination such as racism are of no concern. The privilege that most PR practitioners enjoy in some form or another (e.g. in terms of race, class, cultural capital, income and/or education) is normalized, leaving it unmarked and unremarkable. Clearly, individual practitioners may well be engaged in social causes or recognize the importance of material circumstances, but in their professional role they are not required to bring this awareness to bear on their work. The primacy of the organization as the locus for PR work obscures the ways in which race, gender and class shape the distribution of power both within and outwith the field.

4 Constructing competence
Client, capital and embodiment

If the first 'pillar' of racialization in PR is the erasure of inequity as a parameter for PR practice and knowledge, then the second is the pervasiveness of whiteness throughout the field as a benchmark for practitioner identity. In this chapter my aim is to interrogate the whiteness of the field to reveal how it surfaces as unspoken assumptions about the race, gender and class of PR practitioners, and thus acts as a locus of occupational power (Grimes, 2002). I argue that the way PR discourses construct practitioner identity through the articulation of particular competencies, enhances racialization because of the implicit assumption that the practitioners will be able to claim whiteness as a form of property (Harris, 1993) that they can draw on to demonstrate their 'fit' with the requirements of the field.

I focus in particular on the subjective competencies that are presented as appropriate ways of being in PR discourse, and consider the aspects of whiteness embedded within them. Throughout the discussion, I reflect on how assumptions of whiteness that permeate occupational identity present challenges for BAME practitioners, who must illustrate their fit with the occupational habitus even as their difference is repeatedly called out by the normative understanding of what and who a PR practitioner should be.

Identity, competence and the professionalization project

The articulation of practitioner identity in PR's occupational discourse, like the articulation of practice and knowledge, is not simply a passive description of what already exists, but both constructs and instructs practitioners about the effective embodiment of PR. Discourse constructs subjects by disciplining 'at a distance', prompting compliance through valorizing particular forms of self-management, but without imposing specific forms of control (Foucault, 1991; Miller and Rose, 1990).

Successfully disciplining practitioners into the appropriate demonstration of occupational identity is central to professional projects, since it strengthens the impression of a coherent and unified occupational field by complementing clearly defined knowledge and practice with an identifiable 'professional' and a defined set of competencies. A successful jurisdictional claim by PR, therefore, is dependent not only on approval from external sources of legitimacy, but also on effective, systematic discipline within occupational fields, so that practitioners identify with the occupational archetype and perpetuate it both within the field and to the external world. Hodgson (2002: 806) calls this the 'double-edged nature of professional discipline', where practitioners both govern and are governed by occupational norms.

Practitioners, constructed as a homogenous group rather than individuals, serve as an occupational resource that contributes to the occupation's 'labour of legitimation' (Fournier, 1999: 286), providing evidence of the 'truth' of PR's legitimacy and jurisdiction. Practitioner identity is embedded in occupational discourses as a set of competencies, or explanations of skills and attributes that relate not only to what PR does, but who does it. Competence comprises specialist knowledge and technical skills, but also embodiment and personal conduct (Anderson-Gough *et al.*, 2000; Fournier, 1999), and therefore extends the scope of an archetypal identity beyond practice-specific skills and into the realm of personality, character and values. Competencies, then, call out identity – and vice versa – and articulate what it means to fit in with the occupational group (Evetts, 2011). The workplace, as the location where occupational knowledge is applied in practice by drawing on different competencies, can be understood as a 'site for contestations about the nature of human identity, and for attempts to shape and reshape the identity of individuals' (Miller and Rose, 1995: 428).

The disciplinary logic of PR produces two basic themes that underpin archetypal competencies: the client/consultant relationship, and rationality/emotion at work. Because PR discourses align knowledge and practice so closely with organizations and their requirements, and because the PR workplace frequently is the client organization, competence is constructed in ways that reflect, rather than contrast with, client needs and identities. The result is that the client becomes a measure of competence, invoked as a means of 'responsibilizing' practitioners towards an important source of PR's legitimacy and, in the persona of the happy or unhappy client, a disciplinary measure of 'appropriate' conduct (Du Gay and Salaman, 1992).

Centring the client in constructions of competence ensures that the occupation's dedication to the client and their interests is communicated not only through campaigns that serve client interests, but also embodied by those whose job it is to consult with, advise and accompany the client through the vagaries of the complex environment (Anderson-Gough *et al.*, 2000). Demonstrating homology through embodiment and practice is essential for service occupations, since it engenders trust, loyalty, a more secure client relationship and, ultimately, more business (Hanlon, 1999b). PR's clients are frequently white, since Whiteness is overrepresented at the managerial level in organizations (Atewologun and Singh, 2010; Race for Opportunity, 2010) and it is managers to whom practitioners most often answer. Consequently, while BAME practitioners may be able to draw on some aspects of their identity, such as class or gender, to establish commonality with the client, their bodies, as signifiers of difference (Puwar, 2004; Hall, 1996), are more likely to disturb the perceptions of a neatly aligned client/practitioner partnership, at least in the initial stages of a relationship. For white colleagues, as Carbado and Gulati (2003: 1778) argue, the problem is not the same.

In the context of workplaces that are structured around cooperative work, whites do not have to, in terms of race, think about being the same. They have a limited need to strategize about how and when to signal an integrational capacity to work within teams without causing grit. Whiteness is presumptively grease.

PR's workplaces are also subject to the general historical trend in organizations of separating rationality from emotion in matters of work. Brewis and Grey (1994: 69) note that an emphasis on rationality in 'modernist-masculinist' organizations has led to workplaces where 'emotion, sex and intimacy are to remain at home'. Emotional labour, as controlled and productive emotion, such as demonstrating enthusiasm for one's work, or a nurturing approach to clients and customers, has long been recognized as an important dimension of service industries and occupations, including the media industries (Hesmondhalgh and Baker, 2008; Korczynski, 2003; Hochschild, 1983). However, it may only be exercised within the parameters of delivering a good service; disconnected from this it may become unpredictable and detrimental. In PR, emotional labour is fundamental to how practitioners manage their identities in client and journalist relationships, exemplified in the need to deliver unconditional support for the client, deal calmly with difficult journalists, and present a positive, upbeat image. Such labour is reflected in gendered discourses of caring and supportive relationships, and enacted by a largely female workforce (Surma and Daymon, 2013; Yeomans, 2013; Bridgen, 2011). Yet, the normative position of PR practitioners as members of the 'dominant coalition', requires an emphasis on strategic rationality combined with commercial and political savvy. To realize occupational legitimacy, then, PR competencies need to reflect both rational, analytical capabilities and an emotionally driven commitment to the service relationship; the juggling act is evident in the ways that the subjectivities of client and customer are articulated in its discourses.

The overt emphasis on rationality in the workplace systematically disadvantages women, whose gendered identities have historically belonged to the emotional, domestic sphere and who are therefore perceived as 'more' emotional – and less able to control their emotions – than men (Brewis and Grey, 1994). In addition, it is a potential barrier for BAME PR practitioners to overcome in their day-to-day work, since racial stereotypes are frequently associated with uncontrollable emotion, irrationality, a lack of self-discipline and a tendency to the unpredictable (Hall, 1997). Stereotypes associated with Black women have emphasized their sexuality and promiscuity, as well as their availability for White men in particular (Ladson-Billings, 2009; bell hooks, 1994).

Such barriers would be less of a concern if their effect on practitioner careers was limited. However, subjective competencies associated with personality, attitudes and fit are treated as forms of merit in occupational contexts, even though they do not conform to measurable or objective criteria (assessing how enthusiastic someone is, for example, depends on the subjective interpretation of 'enthusiasm' in relation to a particular individual, rather than objective measures of some kind of technical capability to be enthusiastic). As 'appropriate ways of being' (Fournier, 1999: 296), they provide a 'mechanism of social differentiation and likeness' (Alvesson, 1994: 539) that plays into the competitive struggles for position and power both within PR and between PR and competing fields. As a result, they are central to the occupational habitus as a mechanism which 'synthesises and guides symbolic action' (Alvesson, 1994: 540), and in the context of which discourse exercises its disciplinary effect. The emphasis on personal qualities as forms of merit is further strengthened by the enterprise culture that characterizes many organizations, where 'certain qualities, self-reliance, personal responsibility, boldness, willingness to take risks, are regarded as virtues, and promoted as such' (Du Gay and Salaman, 1992: 628). As a consequence, subjective competencies receive far more attention in the PR texts than technical prowess, being reiterated in different ways and different contexts, while objective forms of merit (qualifications, experience) are limited to recruitment pages or practitioner biographies.

A note on method

The material on which the following discussion is based includes the websites and industry documentation described in Chapter 3. In addition, I draw on material from a critical discourse analysis of 11 practitioner profiles that appeared in the UK edition of *PRWeek* during 2009. The profiles (referenced by date of the issue, page numbers and the first two words of the title) were analysed as part of the same study, and comprised double-page spreads narrating a high-profile practitioner's career. They included a portrait-style picture of the practitioner that took up almost a whole page. The profiles were formulaic in their composition, beginning with a rationale for the profile (the practitioner's current position and success story); followed by a brief career history and personal background; comments from mentors and key business associates; and concluding with reflections from the practitioner and the journalist about future prospects. The profiles also included boxed out 'top tips' for success, and a list of attributes that the practitioner would look for in a young, upcoming practitioner. In other words, the profiles were constructed as both exemplars of best practice, and as sources of insight and expertise on what practitioners should or could do to enhance their career. As such, they provided an insight into the competencies and personality traits that 'fit' PR, exemplify the PR habitus and lead to success. In addition, the final section of the chapter draws on a quantitative analysis of the gender and race represented in all practitioner images published across 18 issues of *PRWeek* from 2009 and 2010.

The ingredients of PR competence

Technical expertise is the 'lowest common denominator of professionalism' (Grey, 1998: 575), but demonstrating it is nonetheless necessary, since it exemplifies the specialist knowledge that is part of PR's claim to a particular jurisdiction. Traditional forms of evidence are certainly presented in the PR texts as necessary forms of individual merit: a good degree is mentioned by consultancies and industry associations as a minimum requirement, and elite universities receive special attention (Yale, Leeds, Cambridge and Oxford, for example). Practitioner biographies also mention track record and industry experience, while all the consultancy websites illustrate their technical capability by listing or detailing case studies of successful campaigns.

In the case studies, technical excellence is illustrated not by descriptions of individual brilliance, but by making success a collective endeavour ('our team'; 'we'), where all practitioners are the (anonymous) architects of success:

- We challenged the United Kingdom to seek weight management advice.
- We developed a global campaign to promote mobile broadband on behalf of the GSMA, leading to the fastest ever adoption of a broadband technology, with over 1,000,000 subscribers in the first three years.
- We're the team that handled all media and stakeholder relations around the largest repatriation of United Kingdom citizens since Dunkirk.

(Hill and Knowlton, 2010)

More general claims focus on practitioners' ability to combine specialist expertise with sector-specific knowledge in ways that deliver organizational outcomes.

> Our dedicated team of investor relations consultants combine backgrounds in investment banking, equity analysis, fund management, accountancy and in-house investor relations to bring an unparalleled breadth of financial markets expertise and an in-depth understanding of the international investment community's IR requirements. Add to that our rigorous analytical skills and extensive access to the buy and sell-side and you start to understand why we are consistently ranked among the leaders in our field.

(CitigateDeweRogerson, 2010)

Listing skills and experience without talking about who implements them, abstracts the role of PR to an objective analytical tool, a resource that can resolve organizational issues. Reifying objectivity as part of PR's technical effectiveness reflects the modernist-masculinist organizational context that Brewis and Grey (1994) describe, where the private sphere should not interfere with the conduct of work. Objectivity suggests authority, the ability to assess situations strategically and offer judgement unsullied by organizational self-interest. The PR persona must be analytical and dispassionate when it comes to problem analysis and resolution, in order to become 'the sort of person who can be trusted with the truth' (Fournier, 1999: 287).

> An impartial perspective is crucial [...]. We give frank and constructive advice to ensure that the positive messages come across clearly.

(Fishburn Hedges, 2010b)

However, as noted above, the notion of the dispassionate, expert practitioner is complicated by the fact that emotional labour is fundamental to successful consulting (Wellington and Bryson, 2001), and therefore, the complete separation of emotion from PR workplaces would significantly limit the effectiveness of consultants. In the texts, emotion is introduced through the construction of archetypal forms of embodiment and personal qualities that ensure the correct performance of PR competence in line with the occupational habitus (Alvesson, 1994). In so doing, the parameters for conduct, as the appropriate public demonstration of competence, are set. Thus the practitioner who behaves in line with the requirements of habitus becomes a desirable source of support, the locus of a meaningful and devoted relationship with clients. Emotional commitment to the client and the role of consultant is communicated through texts that speak of practitioners' passion – for their clients, about the communications industry and about their work. Consultancies explain their success in terms of 'chemistry' (Bell Pottinger, 2010), being 'genuinely different' and even demonstrating 'a touch of magic'.

We are passionate about your business but also about our industry. Passion makes us determined to say yes (Even when the safe answer should be no). [...] Passion's made us ambitious, challenging and honest (We think you're paying for the right response for you, not the easy one for us). [...] Enthusiasm drives you to think the unthinkable, passion drives us to do the un-doable.

(Freud Communications, 2010a)

Passion, chemistry and enthusiasm are presented as a form of collective merit in the texts, but it is practitioners who make up the collective 'we' and are required to make different forms of 'magic' tangible in day to day work. The manifestation of passion and enthusiasm is hard work and unqualified commitment, going 'above and beyond' (Freud Communications, 2010b) ordinary – albeit unspecified – expectations. The translation of collective magic to individual efficacy is made via the medium of intangible 'talent': successful practitioners are described as having an instinct or for communications, a 'flair', or a 'rare' quality that makes the service they provide particularly unique.

Bell Pottinger group chairman Kevin Murray points to Jarvis' flair for strategic thinking: 'Coming out of TV, she is a fast thinker. She is tough but a good listener'.

(230909/16/Defendinghealth)

Globe-Trotter director Gary Bott says: 'Raoul is quite simply one of those rare individuals who understands and respects each and every brand with which he works'.

(061109/16/naturalnetworker)

Demonstrating talent, then, illustrates a practitioner's 'fit' with the occupational field. However, talent can only ever be subjectively assessed, which leaves the door open for processes of racialization to be implicitly reinforced. Those who can claim other archetypal characteristics, such as normative forms of social and cultural capital (see below), embodiment, the flexibility to devote themselves to their client, or the financial and practical wherewithal to network outside office hours, are more likely to be perceived as talented, precisely because they blend in with the field's requirements so well. BAME practitioners may be able to claim many of these characteristics, but their bodies, in contrast to those of their white colleagues, carry the sedimented history of subjugation and prejudice, and do not automatically suggest this kind of identity or capability. Consequently, they usually have to work harder for their talent to be recognized. Their position is likely to be made more difficult by the fact that the field favours practitioners who are modest about their talent. To boast about it would suggest that they feel themselves more important than either the client, or the occupation, and raise doubts about their commitment to both.

> Ferrabee's modesty shines through in the interview. He claims to have 'no recognisable skills except experience'.
>
> (060209/18/redundancyspecialist)
>
> Raoul Shah partied with superstar Beyonce and her husband, rap's first CEO Jay-Z, at this year's Cannes film festival, but you would never guess it, thanks to his super-cool demeanour. When talking about celebrities, he might as well be detailing what brand of breakfast cereal he prefers.
>
> (061109/16/naturalnetworker)

The requirement for modesty can work against BAME practitioners, who may have to actively promote their achievements precisely because talent is not always assessed in the same way for them as it is for their white colleagues (Atewologun and Singh, 2010; Ahmed, 2006; Puwar, 2004). Because talent is subjective, it acts as a racial double-bind for BAME practitioners (Carbado and Gulati, 2013): on the one hand, their talent is less likely to be recognized; on the other, pointing out their achievements may result in them being seen as too pushy, self-interested, arrogant or ambitious. Moreover, the latter characteristics may well be perceived more negatively, given the historical construction of Black and Asian communities in the United Kingdom as subordinate to white political and economic elites, rather than equals, and disruptive rather than exemplary of good practice (see Chapter 2).

According to the industry associations, the person suited to PR has an interest in current trends and events; can rise to any occasion and is confident in the company of a diverse set of people (or, at least, people with a diverse set of occupational backgrounds):

> PR practitioners must be confident talking to a wide range of people – for example, your role may involve presenting to clients, dealing with journalists and meeting with groups of people important to your organisation or client.
>
> (Chartered Institute of Public Relations, 2011a)

You need to be someone who finds it easy to get along with people you don't know and make conversation. Building up a network of contacts is vital if you want to excel in this profession.

(Public Relations Consultants Association, 2009)

The 'networked' professional is able to tap into the social architecture of an occupation 'within and through which both professional knowledge and professional behavior can be transmitted' (Anderson-Gough *et al.*, 2006: 236). The value of networking, then, is not simply an instrumental means of career development or a source of information – indeed, the texts emphasize sociability and breadth of networks rather than targeted contact development. Rather, they are a 'critical framework of meaning' (Anderson-Gough *et al.*, 2006: 252) for practitioners that provides an understanding of how things work in an occupation or workplace. They are, in other words, a means of socializing practitioners into occupational and organizational norms by communicating habitus and cultural capital. Correspondingly, networks are more powerful and have greater longevity when they originate from common formative experiences of occupational socialization, such as professional training (Anderson-Gough *et al.*, 2006).

Breadth of networks leads to breadth of knowledge, but the texts also make it clear that a pre-requisite for 'good networking' is an existing stock of wide-ranging cultural capital; in other words, cultural knowledge is required to access valuable professional knowledge. For clients to feel comfortable, practitioners must be able to converse about a range of topics, from fine wine and shooting to politics, current affairs, or the arts. The ideal, energetic, dynamic and sociable practitioner will be able to 'hit the ground running' (Fishburn Hedges, 2010c) and consequently, will be more successful. In the *PRWeek* profiles, being sociable is presented as evidence of a balanced individual with whom colleagues, employers and clients can feel comfortable, reinforcing the fact that sociability is part of the PR identity.

Whitehorn does not possess the bubbly persona of his boss. On the contrary, he seems rather intense. [...] But an industry insider says 'while there are traces of geekiness about him' he is actually 'a late-night party animal who likes fine wine and shooting'.

(190609/14/galacticenterprise)

Not everyone, however, is equally able to achieve this ideal. The way 'good' sociability is defined in the texts makes it dependent on cultural omnivorousness, or access to and knowledge of a wide range of cultural and social experiences. Research has shown that cultural omniviorousness is associated with elite social groups who have the time, financial wherewithal and educational background that allows them to engage with different activities (Warde and Gayo-Cal, 2009; Peterson and Kern, 1996). If good sociability leads to 'good' networking, and networking leads to important professional knowledge, then practitioners who are less likely to be cultural omnivores stand at a potential disadvantage to their colleagues.

BAME practitioners are vulnerable: even if they demonstrate sociability, they are less likely to have grown up with access to the range of required cultural capital, given that BAME groups are under-represented in both elite educational institutions and elite social strata more generally. While they may learn about or engage in the required activities at a later stage in their lives, they may still lack the easy confidence of their colleagues, born of a habitus that more readily fits the occupation, to socialize and converse about a wide range of topics (Bourdieu, 1991).

Networking is also presented as a means to access important social capital, defined by Bourdieu as 'the actual or potential resources which are linked to possession of a durable network of [...] relationships of mutual acquaintance and recognition [...] which provides each of its members with the backing of the collectively owned capital, a "credential" which entitles them to credit, in the various senses of the word' (Bourdieu, 1997: 51). In PR, social capital relates to networks of professional and personal connections with clients, journalists and other elite influencers that practitioners can leverage to ensure they influence the communications landscape (Ihlen, 2007, 2005). Social capital is implicitly equated with influence and career success, and delivers access to practical knowledge. In the following quote, for example, elite contacts deliver total understanding of 'the system' for one practitioner.

> Allan remains close to his former Downing Street colleagues, many of whom are now in the cabinet. In particular, work and pensions secretary James Purnell was best man at his wedding and remains his closest friend. [...] Many senior journalists also know him well. The Sun's George Pascoe-Watson, a regular golfing chum, says: 'He used to firefight in Downing Street and knows the players – he totally understands the system'.
>
> (150509/16/Leavingblair)

However, deconstructing the meaning of social capital in the field reveals another dimension of the occupation's racializing bias towards elite groups. Not all social capital carries the same weight: elite networks of contacts in other largely white, middle- or upper-class occupations such as politics, law and the media, all bear mention, while non-elite family or work connections are absent from the texts. Privileging elite networks is a means of linking the occupation to other professional groups and shoring up its claims to status, but elite networks are also harder to break into without a personal link, which makes them more difficult for BAME practitioners to access (Puwar, 2004). Entry takes longer and more work, and they are likely to have to justify their position in a way unnecessary for white colleagues. In other words, the normative definition of 'good' social capital is easier for those from elite, largely white groups to fulfil.

Creativity is also reified in the texts as an essential practitioner attribute, and in this PR echoes the advertising industry, where creativity is as much a discursive construction as a material reality, helping practitioners market their services (Alvesson, 1994). As the PRCA explains, 'a successful PR consultant is prepared to take risks and is constantly searching for new innovative and creative ways to give their clients access to the media' (Public Relations Consultants Association, 2009). Because competence is not only about knowledge but also about embodiment, creativity must also be outwardly visible. Success comes from not only delivering creative ideas or unusual campaign strategies, but embodying difference through unusual or elite forms of cultural and social capital. Examples from the texts include high profile personal connections (090109/16/comingin), a grandfather who was an inventor (190609/14/galacticenterprise), or an international upbringing.

> When growing up he went to nine schools, in six cities, in three continents, and he jokes: 'I studied the French revolution three times in two different languages and I still do not know a thing about it'.
>
> (060209/18/redundancyspecialist)

An impressive, but unusual track record in the PR industry, such as experience in the gambling industry (200309/14/easyhospitality) or an international jet-set lifestyle (061109/16/naturalnetworker), also counts as evidence of creativity and an intangible difference that sets a practitioner (and their practice) apart from competitors.

> He played poker with Boyzone and got the Playboy Bunnies to stop traffic in Piccadilly at the same time as writing documents about deregulating the gambling industry. [...] When he was setting up the world's largest poker game it went from the sublime to the ridiculous. I would get a call in the pub and I would be saying things like 'yeah, slims, I'm not sure if the Devil Fish and the Hendon Mob agree with that, but I'll see what I can do'.
>
> (200309/14/easyhospitality)

Such stories suggest that an archetypal practitioner will be able to draw on forms of capital that give them the capacity to bring something new to the client relationship, and echo the breadth of knowledge that a 'good' networker should be able to deploy. However, the capital that receives attention in the texts is associated with elite groups, rather than coming from a more diverse set of social and cultural contexts. Because they are delivered as part of the narrative of a successful career, these elite forms of capital become normalized as attributes that a practitioner both requires and is rewarded for if they want to reach the heights of PR success. In other words, the differential valuation of types of cultural and social capital contributes to the racialization of the field.

The embodied practitioner

The archetypes of occupational knowledge described in Chapter 3, and the competences described in this chapter, constitute important ingredients for the occupational identity required to 'fit' PR's occupational habitus. Habitus is also embodied, however, and identity in PR is also communicated through images of practitioners scattered throughout the texts. While visual representations of PR practitioners do not circulate in the same way that discourses are reproduced intertextually and through conversations and practice, they none-theless provide a reference point for readers that shows what kinds of people tend to be successful or happy in PR, and against which colleagues and oneself can be compared. They are frequently accompanied by descriptions of practitioners, which may include comments about dress or demeanour.

The analysis of 604 practitioner images published across 18 issues of *PRWeek* in 2009 and 2010 was not designed to be an in-depth statistical investigation of the patterns of representation in what remains the most important trade publication for PR in the United Kingdom, but the results do suggest that the visual representation of the archetypal practitioner is overwhelmingly white and male. Two-thirds (69 per cent) of practitioners depicted were male and only 5 per cent were non-white. While the 12 non-white women depicted were all different, the 19 pictures of non-white men represented only eight separate individuals. The proportion of all women prac-titioners depicted in groups (26 per cent) was also higher than that for men (14 per cent), suggesting that women are less frequently represented as an authority or source of expertise. No visible disabilities were represented at all in any of the issues. In the consultancy and industry association websites, the pattern was similar: practi-tioners depicted in the texts are invariably white, able-bodied and their dress (suits, shirts, or casual with no obvious religious dress) suggested a middle-class, secular background. Practitioners are cheerful, smiling and clearly comfortable in their cho-sen field; the reader is left in little doubt that they navigate their organization and client relationships with ease. Senior practitioners also tend to be male.

The *PRWeek* profiles include explicit and gendered comment on practitioners' self-presentation. In the case of women, physical attractiveness and dress was often noted in the introduction to the article, while men were described less often in terms of specific physical attributes; instead, the overall impression they cre-ated, particularly in the context of client interaction, was more of a focus.

> Sian Jarvis [...] is glamorous but perfectly presented in pearls and a smart blouse in her Whitehall office for our interview. [...] But ten years ago, when she started at [the Department of Health], fresh from her political correspondent role at GMTV, her former boss' advice was: 'Wear your leather trousers on the first day'.
>
> (230909/16/Defendinghealth)

> 'He is easy, direct and typically Scottish,' adds Cotton. 'He has not lost his accent or his affection for Scottish football and he is not backwards in say-ing his piece.'
>
> (200309/14/easyhospitality)

When read in conjunction with the discourses about desirable personalities for PR practitioners, these pictures and descriptions communicate the gendered and classed forms of racialization that underpins the field's archetypes. They 'say' that those who find it easiest to be a PR practitioner, those who are best at it, delivering to client expectations, demonstrating intelligence and strategic thought, at once passionate and analytical, able to meet any challenge, are normally white, able-bodied, secular and young. They also suggest that senior PR capabilities are normally found in men, rather than women. They confirm that belonging is not just about personality, having a degree or having worked for particular clients but about race, class and gender as well. In other words, they act as a powerful illustration of the whiteness that structures the occupational field. In the process, they show how those who cannot claim properties associated with whiteness are unlikely to fit in.

Conclusion: whiteness in UK PR

In what ways do the constructions of competence described in this chapter discipline practitioners? On one level, they provide guidance as to what skills and attributes are needed to enter and progress in PR. Degrees, experience and a successful track record are all, perhaps, predictable. In addition, however, the discourses clarify the kinds of behaviour that will be rewarded in the workplace and in work relationships. To prioritize the client and their needs (sometimes 24 hours a day) is good, to be self-interested is not; to be passionate about communication is good, to be indifferent is not; to develop networks and be sociable is good, to prefer quiet nights in is not; to demonstrate intelligence, ambition and creativity is good, to be hands-on, routine and tactical is not. Following Miller and Rose (1990: 18), to the extent that the norms of the field can be translated into these kinds of individual values, decisions and judgments 'they can function as part of [practitioners'] "self-steering" mechanisms'.

The desired behaviours are logical in the context of protecting PR's jurisdiction, its identity and its claim to a particular form of expertise. The frequency with which they are reiterated normalizes them as part of the occupational doxa, and makes them seem unproblematic. After all, in a world that ignores inequity, in principle any practitioner from any background is able to demonstrate total dedication, creativity, and access to networks in the ways described here. The idea of 'difference' or diversity within the practitioner body, understood as a political issue, rarely appears in the documents because there is no requirement for it. Where diversity does appear in relation to individual practitioners, it is a way of describing their communications experience (they have worked in a wide range of sectors or for a wide range of clients) or professional background (as journalists, bankers, healthcare professionals), and suggests a high level of skill and social capital, both of which benefit the client. Positive formulations of diversity are driven by the desire to demonstrate creativity and breadth of experience, and are followed by reassurances that practitioners are 'united' or connected, still part of 'our people' who have a passion for communications:

> Our people are an eclectic bunch, with diverse backgrounds including advertising, research, journalism, banking, politics, consultancy and in-house communications. All are united by a passion and flair for communications, as well as a sense of hard-work and fun.
>
> (Fishburn Hedges, 2010a)

This 'creative diversity' divorces the idea of diversity from political (and therefore troublesome) notions of identity and (in)equality (Malik, 2013), and shifts attention to client-centred questions of quality, ensuring that creativity, skill and social capital remain harnessed in the service of the client.

The archetypal identities that emerge from PR's disciplinary logic seem commonsensical for an occupation that is inextricably linked to the organizations in which it operates, where the environment is defined in narrow, organizational terms, and where social inequality is ignored. The competencies that count if practitioners want to be successful, must be framed in terms that are relevant to organizational interests. The figure of the client looms large: practitioners must be dedicated to their client or employing organization, doing whatever is necessary to ensure the client is satisfied. They must also be similar to the client, sharing interests or at least demonstrating an interest in their interests, socializing and making the client feel comfortable.

This is PR's version of a 'politics of racelessness', where 'community, access and inclusion are implied, but it is the arguments of the market state [...] which are declared through the new economy of creativity' (Mailk, 2013: 238). Occupational archetypes decontextualize and depoliticize identity and thereby hold PR's particular form of whiteness in place as a universal signifier that 'strives to structure all social identities' (Sharma and Sharma, 2003: 306). However, the archetypes are problematic because they valorize subjective attributes and behaviours that are not available to everyone, or have the potential to be differently evaluated for racialized, gendered and classed individuals. Socializing outside working hours, for example, or working long hours to deliver extra value, assume a flexible home life, financial resources to fund social engagements, and, frequently, a liberal approach to drinking alcohol, all of which can exclude practitioners with responsibilities at home, financial constraints or particular religious beliefs. Not everyone has elite family connections that they can use to demonstrate their individuality and the quality of their networks. And intangible, embodied assets such as 'creativity', 'talent' and a 'passion' for communications, which all evoke the image of energetic and inspirational colleagues with innate ability, can only be assessed subjectively. White practitioners, whose raced and classed identities occupy positions of dominance and assumed superiority in British history, enjoy the benefit of 'condensed subjectivities' that orient others towards them as a good 'fit', while BAME practitioners are more likely to have to argue their case explicitly and must provide more extensive evidence to justify their presence and promotion.

Thus, archetypal practitioner identities have the potential to marginalize BAME practitioners both directly and indirectly because they are dependent on a particular formulation of whiteness, the manifestation of the systemic racialization of the field. Whiteness is the 'grease' that makes it easier to move through the PR field (Carbado and Gulati, 2003). It is articulated as merit, a slippery, apparently objective construct that implies success is a result of individual effort but where, in practice, effort is assessed differently for insiders and outsiders (Chang, 2002). Some ways of being different from the norm are valued because they suggest creativity, innovation and talent, but success also depends on demonstrating elite forms of capital, that white, middle-class or upper-class British people (who make up the majority of clients as well as the majority of PR practitioners) can access more easily. BAME practitioners are less likely than their white British colleagues to access the forms of capital that the occupation valorizes. Moreover, the narrow focus on organizations and objectivity means that the insights BAME practitioners might have as a result of their experiences of being in a group that faces discrimination and disadvantage in wider society, are irrelevant to the occupation or difficult to voice. Consequently, as a general rule, those who can lay claim to whiteness as a property will find it easier to fit into the occupation, and will be perceived to fit more readily, because their backgrounds allow them to claim the archetypal identities and knowledge that define the occupation and legitimize its jurisdictional claims.

This is not to say that all white practitioners will fit more readily in the occupational field, nor that all BAME practitioners will be marginalized. Identity is intersectional: it relates not only to race or ethnicity, but also to other forms of privilege/discrimination such as class and gender, which will interact with race and ethnicity to position individuals in the field. Some BAME practitioners may be able to draw on a privileged class background which means their race is not a difference that 'matters' unless it is called out in a particular circumstance. Similarly, some white practitioners may be disadvantaged by their class or gender in different contexts. The point about archetypal practitioner competencies and identities is that they comprise a system of *normative* parameters that structure hierarchies within the field, and must be negotiated by all members. Their systemic nature gives rise to repeated instances or events where BAME practitioners are put at a potential disadvantage compared with their white colleagues – or, in Coates' (2006) terms, where their 'race' is constructed anew and their identities racialized. In contrast to the grease that whiteness provides, being Black or Asian constitutes a form of 'grit' that can cause friction (Carbado and Gulati, 2003).

This and the previous chapter have illustrated how PR's corporate professionalization project, as an exercise in securing status and legitimacy for the occupation, constructs occupational knowledge and practice, as well as practitioner competence and identity, in ways that reflect whiteness as a marketable, commercially attractive set of properties that means white, middle-class practitioners are more likely to be successful in the field. However, a dialectical approach to analysing the field reminds us that this is only half the story. Marginalized practitioners will not simply accept the field's prescriptions, but will challenge and work with them in ways that help them realize their own ambitions alongside, or in spite of, occupational priorities. In Chapter 5, the voices of BAME PR practitioners themselves reveal the ways they see, understand and contest the field's doxa, habitus and archetypes in order to successfully pursue their chosen career.

5 Strategies of resistance

Intersectional identities as a source of critique

The systemic racialization that marks PR's doxa and habitus is not the whole story of the professional experience for BAME practitioners; their responses to imposed subjectivities are an essential to how their careers evolve. Managing their identity is always and inevitably a political struggle for voice, visibility and belonging in PR. The resources they draw on come from both the occupational context itself, and from their lives outside work. To grasp the full picture of diversity in PR in the United Kingdom, we need to understand not only which resources practitioners use to resist exclusion, but also how and when they use them, and for what purpose.

As explained in Chapter 2, the history of racialization in the United Kingdom generates subjectivities for BAME practitioners that are marked by essentialist preconceptions about their intellect, skills, literacy, physicality and sexuality relative to white colleagues. They are constructed as objects whose meaning is partly predetermined ('less intelligent', 'untrustworthy', 'lazy', 'sexual predator') and situates them 'appropriately' in relation to their colleagues (Hylton, 2009; Ladson-Billings, 2009; Gillborn, 2008). Postcolonial research reminds us that the process of 'othering' is manifest through (in)visibility (Spivak, 1988), and Ahmed (2012, 2006) argues that these preconceptions are materialized in the workplace through variable orientations towards the 'other' who somehow embodies the burden of difference and is more or less visible at different times. Orientations are a legacy of how the right to enter and belong in particular spaces, including occupational fields, has been constructed historically. In the context of PR, as an occupation in which both doxa and habitus privilege whiteness, the historical subjectivities that BAME practitioners carry with them construct them as the 'outsider-within' the field. Colleagues may turn towards them for certain forms of expertise (e.g. the ability to understand the communications needs of a particular community, or to access a particular segment of the media), but turn away from them when needs relate to an area where they do not 'belong', or are not expected to be present (e.g. when appointing a new CEO, or a company spokesperson).

Insofar as hegemonic discourses and practices of 'othering' remove the grounds for her inclusion, when the 'other' becomes visible to 'insiders' (usually white PR practitioners), their presence is therefore a permanent surprise. They are perceived as the cause of uncertainty and even fear; the encounter becomes awkward. Insiders must negotiate their way around the 'new' presence, a process that 'causes disruption, necessitates negotiation, and invites complicity' (Puwar, 2004: 1). The situation is further complicated by the fact that the 'other' throws into relief the homogeneity that results from privileging whiteness; the stark difference in the presence and authority of outsiders-within and insiders, cannot be explained away by skills-based narratives of merit. Consequently, in making privilege and difference visible, the 'other' undermines merit as a legitimizing discourse of objectivity (Puwar, 2004). The presence of the 'other' can be understood as heretical to the field, in the same way that Bourdieu (2000) explains heretical discourse as a fundamental challenge to the habitus, shaking the foundations of a particular world-view. In PR, it does not take much for a BAME practitioner to symbolize heresy: their presence alone has the potential to disturb the occupational legitimacy and symbolic power of whiteness. Constituting a heretical presence is one aspect of the grit that the racialized BAME practitioner must minimize if they want to make progress.

To negotiate a path through the workplace, BAME practitioners manage what Carbado and Gulati (2013) call 'workplace identity'. Carbado and Gulati point out that the incentive to hire and promote individuals who embody diversity is contingent on the costs associated with having them in the organization (Carbado and Gulati, 2003), costs which are often inferred based on the ways in which the 'other' manages their identity in ways that are racially palatable, while avoiding behaviour that might trigger negative associations. Likening the organization to a theatrical performance, they argue that, in the North American context, fitting into predominantly white organizations requires African Americans to act out a 'racial double-bind' on a daily basis. As they put it (2013: 1): 'The main characters are white. There are one or two blacks in supporting roles. Survival is always in question. The central conflict is to demonstrate that one is black enough from the perspective of the supporting cast and white enough from the perspective of the main characters'. While all employees have to manage their working identities to some degree, the existence of negative racial stereotypes provides an additional incentive for racialized employees to engage in identity management in order to be able to pursue their careers (Atewologun and Singh, 2010; Kirton, 2009).

Carbado and Gulati (2013) identify a number of ways in which racialized 'others' manage their identity. Racial comforting describes the ways that individuals attempt to make insiders feel comfortable around their presence, and involves emphasizing aspects of their lives that appeal to insiders, while minimizing differences and avoiding politicized discussions of race or difference. Strategic passing involves downplaying racial identity by avoiding activities that might trigger expectations of difference, such as associating with other black people, or speaking a different language. Alternatively, individuals might explicitly declare their liking for stereotypically white, middle-class activities such as (in the United Kingdom) theatre-going, skiing, or sailing. Sometimes, exploiting stereotypes might be a useful strategy to secure a particular career advantage (e.g. by demonstrating in-depth knowledge about how to communicate with a particular ethnic community), and providing discomfort (e.g. speaking out about discrimination) may be useful if debate is valued in a particular institution as evidence of being a 'good' citizen. In contrast, some individuals may choose to adapt completely to the occupational or organizational habitus and argue that discrimination does not exist, to the benefit of their own career but to the detriment of other 'outsiders'. To the extent that this and/or other strategies, such as strategic passing, mark individuals as not 'black enough', however, they may adopt 'buy-back' strategies, arguing the corner for other 'outsiders' on certain occasions.

These strategies are likely to be equally relevant to BAME professionals in the United Kingdom who, as outsiders-within their fields, occupy liminal space from which they can use their 'double-consciousness', or knowledge of different institutions and ideologies (e.g. occupational fields, whiteness, professionalism, racism) to negotiate their position (Atewologun and Singh, 2010; Holvino, 2008; Acker, 2006; King, 1988). Hurtado (1996: 375–376) describes this as 'successful marginality' based on a 'shifting consciousness' that draws on the 'unique knowledge that can be gleaned from the interstices of multiple and stigmatized social identities', allowing individuals to manage their own identity and others' responses to it. The degree of success will vary: extracting benefits from liminality is dependent on the cultural, social and economic capital available to individuals that help them understand their position and the mechanisms through which it might be negotiated (Rollock, 2012; Sommerlad, 2009). It is likely, however, that outsiders-within in PR and other white-collar and professional occupations, have at their disposal a good deal of cultural, social, and economic capital derived from their education, income, professional networks, and the symbolic power associated with their occupation, all of which may be used to resist exclusion. Existing research shows that individuals in organizations actively draw on these forms of capital to negotiate the discursive and material constraints of inequality regimes to construct positive identities. In addition, they draw on organizational rules, processes, practices, and language as a set of resources for negotiating their identities in ways that both sustain and resist inequality (Boogard and Roggeband, 2010; Atewologun and Singh, 2010; Zanoni and Janssens, 2007; Acker, 2006). Alternatively, they may set up their own businesses, drawing on their professional and personal capital (in the form of networks, reputation, and specialist knowledge), or they may conform, assuming the occupational archetype and minimizing the impact of their race in work contexts (Edwards, 2013; Ford and Appelbaum, 2009; Tindall, 2009; Pompper, 2004), 'performing' whiteness (Alexander, 2004) to ensure they can pursue and access the same rewards as their colleagues.

Overall, in occupational contexts, the ability to correctly 'read' the occupational doxa and habitus; to demonstrate normative, but arbitrary, forms of merit; to recognize the self-interest that drives the occupation; and to understand the variable role that one is expected to play as the embodiment of diversity, are all important skills that can facilitate career success and security for outsiders-within trying to enact successful marginality. From this perspective, PR's occupational doxa, habitus and archetypes are not only mechanisms of racialization, as discussed in Chapters 3 and 4, but are also (workplace) identity resources that BAME practitioners may draw on, just as their colleagues do, as they make their way through their careers. In addition, the particular epistemo-logical histories of agency and resistance in racialized communities provide specific forms of capital and narratives of belonging that can counter discourses of inferiority and exclusion (Yosso, 2005). It is important to note that conform-ity with discourse and habitus does not equate to capitulation; it may be a pragmatic choice that allows an individual to be more certain of realizing their ambitions. Conforming and working hard to succeed despite barriers can be, and often is, constructed as a way of proving the system wrong (Mirza, 2006). However, successful marginality involves compromise as well as liberation, because it requires that individuals buy into and cooperate with a system that inherently disadvantages them (Balaji, 2009; Carbado and Gulati, 2003).

This is not to say that managing workplace identity comes without a cost. It takes work, it can be painful, and it is complex. In PR, for example, research shows that racialized practitioners may choose to withdraw from difficult encounters and environments, accepting the associated cost in terms of their visibility and appar-ent 'fit' with the organization or occupation. The existence of multiple stereotypes mean that a strategy to address one (e.g. a black female PR practitioner minimizing the risk of being seen in sexualized terms by avoiding late after-work drinks) may result in another being triggered (the assumption that she prefers to socialize with other black friends rather than her white colleagues). Strategies are situation-dependent, not universally available in all contexts and may be contested (Carbado and Gulati, 2013). The need to strategize is also ongoing; as Hall (1996) notes, identity work does not necessarily transfer across different situations. The need to re-establish an effective workplace identity arises anew with each new situation. In other words, individual agency has its limits. The ongoing process of negotiat-ing one's position is always framed by the ways in which racialization in PR attaches certain subjectivities to BAME practitioners that their white colleagues do not have to negotiate.

Nonetheless, Ahmed (2007b) points out that engaging in diversity does contain the possibility of change, however remote, and in occupational fields we are deal-ing with a relational context; the PR field's elite organizations and individuals, and those on the margins, must all shift and change their positions as they interact. By reinterpreting hegemonic discourse and practice, BAME practitioners can trans-form their meaning and alter the space available for articulating and justifying their role and contribution (Zanoni and Janssens, 2004). It is the dialectic between individual and institution that ultimately shapes experience, identity and power.

A note on method

The material in this chapter and the next is drawn from 35 interviews and seven focus groups with 50 BAME PR practitioners, as well as from eight diaries with up to ten entries per person, completed by some of the same practitioners over a 10-week period. The practitioners were recruited using two methods: with a direct invitation

(Continued)

(Continued)

emailed to them after I had seen them featured in *PRWeek*, and through an appeal for participants mailed to the CIPR membership database. I did not pre-determine which ethnic groups should be included in the study, but interviewed all those who responded to the calls for participation, given that they responded as participants who felt marginalized on the basis of their racial or ethnic identity. This meant that a wide range of ethnicities was represented in the study (see Table 5.1): Seventeen participants were male and 33 female. The participants worked either in-house or as consultants across a wide range of sectors, including government, charities, cultural institutions, and commercial organizations. Their experience ranged from 6 months to 30 years.

Each data collection method had a slightly different focus. The interviews allowed practitioners to tell their own stories about how they came to work in PR, and how they felt their ethnicity and personal background had affected the development of their career alongside other aspects of their identity. Focus group participants were asked to describe 'typical' PR practitioners, compare the archetype with their own identities, and consider the consequent advantages and disadvantages they faced in relation to practitioners who more easily fitted the occupational norm. In their diaries, participants recorded reflections about specific occasions when they felt different from the professional norm. The data did not indicate any differences in experience by sector, but the organizational context was important: some practitioners felt that consultancies were less diverse and more difficult for minority practitioners to navigate than in-house environments, and a few noted that discrimination might differ depending on both sector and the attitude of management.

A commonly agreed principle of intersectionality research is that different social categories may have patterns of disadvantage in common, but they are not reducible to each other and their effects are not universally applicable across all situations, because they are shaped by the specific circumstances that have produced a particular site of investigation (Yuval-Davis, 2006; Gunaratnam, 2003; King, 1988). Moreover, Anthias (2013) makes the important point that categories themselves, as discursive, heuristic devices used for particular purposes, may not correspond to the concrete social divisions that exist on the ground; indeed, the latter change as intersectionality is manifested at different times and in different places. Thus, while

Table 5.1 Research participant ethnic identities (self-ascribed)

Ethnicity	Number of participants
Black/Black British/Black Caribbean	16
Indian/British-Indian	14
Pakistani/British-Pakistani	7
Nigeria/unspecified African origin	4
Polish	2
Chinese	2
Welsh	2
Jewish	1
Arabic	1
Mixed heritage	1

social categories are central to intersectional analyses, they should be treated with a degree of suspicion because of their potential to essentialize and reproduce systems of domination. I adopted McCall's (2005) intercategorical approach to intersectionality in my analysis of practitioner interviews, focus groups, and diaries, using race, gender, and class as useful analytical constructs to explain the complex relationships between groups and individuals, but treating the social judgements derived from them with suspicion.

Carbado and Gulati's strategies can be applied to the four analytical levels recommended by Yuval-Davis as a focus for intersectional research: the organizational level (how do racialized 'others' respond to and change organizational structures and processes?); intersubjective level (how do they adjust the ways in which they engage with colleagues to manage their identity?); the experiential level (how do they experience the process of managing their workplace identity?); and the representational level (how do their actions contest or sustain the ideologies of difference that mark the habitus, discourses, and practices of the institution in which they work?). These levels of analysis frame the discussion that follows here and in Chapter 6. I begin with the representational level, and the ways in which the ideology of whiteness is deconstructed and revealed by the participants in the study.

Strategizing for space: responding to whiteness

As a form of systemic racialization, the power of whiteness as a criterion for belonging in PR lies in its reiteration across discourse and practice. It becomes normalized in the habitus as an occupational archetype and acts as a form of discipline for practitioners. The racial stereotypes that form part of the conditions of arrival for BAME PR practitioners, grounded in perceptions of race as a category, and identity as fixed rather than fluid, make it much harder for them to achieve whiteness. Nonetheless, the simple fact of them being present in the field has the potential to change the way their identities are constructed, because it forces the application of an abstract stereotype onto a specific, located individual and reveals it as a fiction. In the process, the meaning and relevance of their race as a factor in their occupational identity is continually redefined.

In fact, resisting exclusion began with participants' deconstruction of the grounds on which it was justified: the implicit and explicit superiority of whiteness. Drawing on insights derived from their liminal position as outsiders-within the occupation, they created doubt about the validity of PR's doxa and habitus, and revealed the flaws and inconsistencies that emerged when whiteness, which they recognized as an ideological position, was applied in practice. The process disempowered those who both prescribe and 'fit' the archetype, and positioned BAME voices centre-stage.

For example, the fact that the vast majority of their colleagues were white and middle-class, and the fact that they repeatedly found themselves to be the only person of colour in the room, whether in an office setting, at networking events and social occasions, around a board table, or with clients, were not taken as evidence that white, middle-class people were better at PR, based on some kind of objectively measured merit. On the contrary, participants were quick to observe how merit functioned in a very different way depending on who it was being applied to. The most striking articulations of this came in the focus groups. Participants were asked to draw a picture of the 'typical' PR practitioner and list the occupational assets and liabilities associated with that identity. As Figure 5.1 shows, the people they drew, and the assets they described, reflected the reality that those whose race and class intersected to provide the objective and subjective forms of merit described in the previous chapters, tended to dominate the field.

The pictures, which reflected the gendered archetypal identity of PR in that they almost always depicted a young, female practitioner, were accompanied

Figure 5.1 (A–D) 'Typical' PR practitioners, as drawn by focus group participants

by notes about the individual's education (never a PR degree), their family background, their financial situation and, frequently, accessories that reflected status, such as a fast car, a smartphone or a bottle of champagne. Networking featured strongly – these people went out a lot, were confident, well-connected with the media and 'in the know' about the industry. Some pictures included depictions of support from (a white, liberal) family or from professional mentors.

Practitioners recognized that the education, race and class of typical PR practitioners helped them by giving them access to cultural and social capital that acted as 'grease' to enhance their fit with the occupational habitus, ease their working relationships and facilitate their careers. In other words, practitioners contested occupational discourses representing whiteness as universally available, by revealing the conditions that made whiteness possible, making visible the race and class bias inherent in the occupational habitus (see Table 5.2).

Table 5.2 Assets and liabilities in PR, typical practitioners

Assets	Liabilities
Race/gender/class	
White (young girl or male)	Family responsibilities
Middle-class/good upbringing	
Cultural/social/economic capital	
(Privileged) university education	None stated
Informed – reads newspapers/ magazines	
Interesting background story	
Financial wealth	
Good connections, PR industry/media friends give access to PR	
Social and cultural fit gives easier access/easier progression in PR	
Mentor – senior male already in the profession	
Has a plan B	
Supportive friend/family/partner with similar career	
Single	
Embodiment	
Appearance/fashionable/well-dressed (short skirt, low-cut top)/attractive	None stated
More like the person interviewing them	
Personality/attitude	
Sharp mind	Mask, fake, not trusted, lack of
Tenacity, ambition	substance, not taken seriously
Strong attitude, confident, outgoing	Temper, stubborn, aggressive, arrogant,
Social skills	pushy, too ambitious

(Continued)

Table 5.2 (Continued)

Assets	Liabilities
PR skills/abilities	
Adaptability, will do anything to fit in, 'all-rounder'	Narrow focus:
Communication skills, persuasive	• Not interested in PR outside their role – unless they want to move into it
Technology skills	• Not interested in targeting anyone who is not white
International clients	
	Lack of experience/too young/career path was too easy/over-indulged
	• Can't cope with uncontrolled events (e.g. uncontrollable news)
	• Can't cope with difficult clients, difficult journalists
	Harder work than they anticipated/more responsibility than they can cope with
	Narrow/distorted/UK-centric assumptions about the world
	Don't develop skills after their degree
Networks	
Networking skills	Not familiar or comfortable with people unlike them
Lively social life	
Drinks alcohol	Not grounded in reality (real life/real friends)

Their critique reinforced the fact that, for typical practitioners, specific skills were less important for success than the forms of capital they enjoyed as an accident of birth.

> [B]eing from a minority background we don't have well established like a long kind of family lineage in this country [...] in terms of them being able to reach back and draw on a body of knowledge, I mean, that for me is one of the reasons why you've got so many more white kids going into Oxbridge, for example, because they're mostly related to someone who went, so they can go to them and say, 'How do I get through the interview?' I don't have that because I don't know anyone, never mind being related to someone, you know, I don't know anyone like that. [...] So we might have really close family ties but in terms of moving anywhere professionally, I think families of an ethnic minority, it's going to take several generations before we're on a par with ... like the established English families here.
>
> (Angela)

The fact that typical practitioners enjoyed 'accidental' success rather than earning it on merit, made space for an additional critique. Because whiteness did not require evidence of genuine ability, it lacked substance; behaviours associated with whiteness were regarded as a mode of rhetoric that acted as a substitute for knowledge (Grey, 1998). The inconsistent connection between genuine merit and career success not only allowed participants to cast doubt on the discourse of a field with 'unparalleled' openness (Public Relations Consultants Association, 2009), but also raised questions about the abilities of typical PR practitioners, whose skills were potentially limited. They were described as 'fake', 'over-confident', full of 'hot air', without adequate experience and unable to understand the lives of people beyond their immediate experience. Such characteristics were constructed as liabilities that could result in individuals progressing too fast, without the skills necessary for more senior positions and without the ability to communicate effectively in an increasingly diverse environment. As Terrie put it, 'they might not have had a lot of experience, they'd done this job for like a year, but then yeah, we like them and they can be promotable. They could probably do about 40 per cent of the job and that was fine'. In the view of the participants, the fact that white practitioners were not always required to prove themselves before they were promoted ironically led to greater doubt about their ability the more senior they became. Moreover, and contrary to occupational discourses promoting the universal applicability of PR, whiteness introduced a clear limitation to the occupation's effectiveness in certain situations.

> How would they know what it's like to be a young Muslim guy, you step onto the Tube and you just happen to have a backpack because you're going to college and people are like freaking out around, post 2001. How is a ... a person from a nice, kind of safe, middle class, home counties background doing a press release in the Home Office about their counter terrorism measures – how are they going to understand how he feels?
>
> (Priya, focus group 4)

While participants argued that the absence of objective merit (skills, experience) was a problem for the individual typical practitioner, they recognized that it did not matter either to the occupation, which promoted archetypal forms of 'fit' as merit, or to the managers and colleagues in organizations who were responsible for recruitment and promotion decisions: 'I have never seen a recruiter of a diverse background [...] It's just much easier for them to place people who look and are like them. And to be honest, PR recruitment is very, it's very blond' (Mavis, focus group 7). On the contrary, participants observed that being able to claim various aspects of whiteness in PR not only meant that 'fit' overshadowed ability as a form of merit, but also that poor skills, or limited skills, were frequently overlooked.

The occupational privilege that whiteness delivered to those who could claim it was in stark contrast to the 'othering' it imposed on those who could never demonstrate the same level of 'fit' with the occupational norm. As explained in Chapter 3, the absence of social context in occupational discourses meant that the possibility of occupational bias in favour of white, middle-class practitioners was written out of PR's habitus. In other words, the habitual orientation of the field towards or away from different types of

Table 5.3 Assets and liabilities in PR, research participants

Assets	Liabilities
Race/gender/class	
None stated	Working class
	Ethnicity/cultural background
	Young, black male
Cultural/social/economic capital	
University education	State education
Understanding of different cultures/Offer a new angle to things/no previous connection to PR/diverse background and experiences gives me better insight	Age (too old/too young)
	Religion (Christian/Muslim)
	Don't like sport (if male)
	Cultural barriers
	Pressure to fit in
Youth/age	
Understanding partner/family	
Financially stable	
Embodiment	
Identifiable because I look different/stand out/name is different	Articulation/accents
Well-spoken	
Personality/attitude	
Confidence/resilient	Perceived to be aggressive, arrogant
Driven/ambitious/determined	
Independent/self-starter	Straight talking, no time-wasting
Hard-working/focused	Lack of confidence/worry about mistakes
Nice person	
Calm/common sense	Bad experiences/take things personally
Grounded in real life	Over-focus on process
	Principled – stick to my views and don't lie
	Non-drinker
PR Skills/abilities	
International clients/accounts	Lack of time/work-life balance
Experience/portfolio/successful track record	Lacking specific skills/experience
Good communicator/persuasive	Low expectations/poor managers/ negative attitude of others
Creative/resourceful/have good ideas	Organizational culture/negative attitude to communications and communications staff
Organized	
Meet deadlines/reliable	
Planner	
Attention to detail	
Good manager	
Strategic/clear thinker	
Specialist knowledge	
Company support and training	
Networks	
Social skills/good networker/good industry networks	Industry/media contacts/hard to build contacts
Media background/contacts	Poor networker/not interested in networking
	No family connections

practitioners (Ahmed, 2006) was masked by the lack of language available to express either discrimination or favoritism. For many participants, whiteness manifested as a master narrative (Solorzano and Yosso, 2002) that excluded 'other' representations of PR; it colonized by silencing them and negated their experience (Spivak, 1988). However, once voice was restored, as it was in this research, the space to speak enabled participants to recount and share their experiences, making discrimination visible and 'writing' it back into structures, practices and discourses.

For example, they discussed how the objective forms of merit available to them were always in danger of being offset by the limitations they faced in terms of 'fit'. When the focus group participants were asked to describe their own assets and liabilities, their responses reversed the aforementioned pattern. Their assets were frequently focused on education, experience, skills, personality, and their ability to engage productively in a wide range of situations – for the most part, more substantive, evidence-based forms of merit than their white colleagues. But almost invariably, their ethnicity, lack of elite cultural and social capital and differences in their education were noted as disadvantages (Table 5.3).

Deconstructing whiteness was not only a discursive process that took place in the research setting. Participants also described how, on a regular basis, they reinterpreted the normative meaning attached to experiences where their difference resulted in 'othering'. For example, Monica had just completed an internship programme specifically for diverse practitioners, where the training included instruction about how to embody whiteness. While it was presented as a set of skills to be acquired, she interpreted it as a means of reinforcing the superiority of whiteness and its class roots, highlighting the negative value associated with her own 'difference' and the fact that it was not an 'appropriate way of being' in PR (Fournier, 1999).

> I think [PR] started with the whites and they, they said that's the standard, that you have to be polished, that you have to come from this background [...]. [At the] internship, it was about, you know, even how to talk, just the mannerism, how to talk, how to conduct ourselves in meetings and that, that's when it becomes a reality how different you are and you're told that if you have to fit you have to start consciously getting to that mannerism to get there and feel comfortable and fit in, otherwise you will always feel like an outsider.
>
> (Monica, focus group 1)

Being taught how to embody the archetypal identity did not make Monica feel more confident; on the contrary, it simply made the prospect of a career in PR seem even more remote. For her, it seemed impossible to learn to embody something that she was not, reflecting Bourdieu's view that the easy familiarity of those who are inculcated with certain forms of cultural and social capital is hard to replicate if you acquire such capital later in life (Bourdieu, 1991, 1984). Yet not learning the visceral forms of whiteness required by PR apparently constituted a non-negotiable barrier to entry; as a means of social differentiation (Alvesson, 1994) that could not be overcome, they were particularly strong barriers to inclusion.

The process of 'othering' that Monica relates also has echoes of colonial dominance, in that it includes making Monica aware of her difference and making her difference 'matter' (Fanon, 2008 [1952]). Her body was marked and defined as inadequate by those training her, who had the power to 'know' and categorize her inadequacies (as the 'other') in the same way that colonial powers defined and 'knew' those who were colonized (Said, 1995). Indeed, the inferiority imposed by racialization was noted particularly among practitioners who had migrated to the United Kingdom, and felt the impact of their difference even more keenly than others, both in general terms as well as in assumptions about their skills and intellect.

> The stereotype starts from when they meet me and hear my voice and know that … hear my accent and know that yes this is an African. So even before they get the opportunity to see me work and evaluate the quality of my output, they already have a stereotype.
>
> (Thomas)

> [W]e have a training budget and they were asking what kind of training would I like to have, and, well, writing press releases? Not really, because I've been doing this for like for how many years and I've written more press releases than some people here […] Anyway I said that one of the things I might want to do is having pronunciation classes or something. So actually my training budget didn't go to PR but to language classes.
>
> (Amy)

The experience of Amy and Thomas illustrates the importance of accent and voice as embodied indicators of difference (Bourdieu, 1991). They were recognized by participants as an important factor in the 'othering' they experienced, and the disciplinary impact of the requirement for an 'appropriate' articulation is evident in the way that Amy regards language classes as a perfectly legitimate form of skills training: she knows that the outcomes of improving her accent would be beneficial in the same way as improving her practical skills might be. The two strategies are fundamentally different, however, in that training in specific skills addresses deficient *occupational* knowledge, while improving accent or language indicates a recognition that one's *embodied* identity is deficient in the context of the field, and must be managed. In this way, the disciplinary effect of whiteness prompts her to know herself as whiteness 'knows' her, and acknowledge her own inadequacies (Fanon, 2008(1952)).

Participants also challenged whiteness by reinterpreting the discomfort that their presence prompted as a result of their colleagues' ignorance rather than their own 'difference'. They recognized the fact that colleagues who did not 'have [diversity] in their lives' (Chary, focus group 5) relied on stereotypes as familiar and manageable points of orientation, assumptions about their intellect, experience and skill that were made before participants had had a chance to demonstrate their capability. Consequently, participants were able to reject any suggestion that stereotypes were some kind of essential 'truth'. Instead, they were regarded as necessary fictions that supported their colleagues' inadequate experience of diversity. Participant identities were marked by recognizable postcolonial subjectivities: they knew they were perceived to be less intellectually capable, less strategic, less suited to leadership, and less reliable than their white colleagues, but their comments suggested that this was because white colleagues had very little contact with people from different ethnic groups. Ignorance was betrayed by the reactions they encountered when stereotypes were overturned, invariably causing palpable surprise: 'They're like "oh you did go to university" and "oh you're not the tea boy," that kind of thing' (Andy, focus group 3).

Some participants talked about the painful experience of this everyday racism (Essed, 1991) – hesitations that suggest surprise and adjustment, 'looks' that linger a microsecond too long, or being looked past – and the corresponding pressure to resist its disempowering effects as colleagues physically or metaphorically turned away from them.

> It's little slights, it's in the meeting room where they don't hear what you say. It's all the little things that they do which are incredibly subtle but still just as undermining and there to kind of make you feel as if they don't really want you there in the room.
>
> (Katy, focus group 2)

These racial 'microaggressions' (Sue *et al.*, 2007)[1] frequently persisted even when participants' job title and budgetary responsibility should have given them recognizable and undeniable authority; the remarkable strength of whiteness as an ideological lens meant that stereotypes were upheld even in the face of contradictory evidence. A racialized subjectivity was 'reimposed' on participants regardless, to ensure that their difference mattered (Sommerlad, 2009, 2008b; Flintoff *et al.*, 2008). Peers would instinctively orient away from the BAME senior manager and towards a white colleague, whom they assumed would have decision-making responsibility. Again, participants did not accept the normative interpretation of their identity as inherently less authoritative, but instead argued that the cause of these reactions was the reluctance of colleagues to both see and accept 'other' bodies as a locus of superiority, leadership and strategic decision-making. They recognized their colleagues' bafflement when the 'other' has 'made himself just as knowledgeable. With him, the game [of inferiority] cannot be played' (Fanon, 2008(1952): 23). The required distance between whiteness and the 'other' was breached in these contexts, and the identification with whiteness that is required for acceptance into PR tipped over to threatening 'subaltern mimicry' that contested the occupational doxa. As Sharma and Sharma (2003: 307) put it, the '*narcissistic* mode of racial authority and power dependent on a know-able and controllable Other [...] slips easily into fear and paranoia for the white subject, when the Other is not in its proper place (no longer "Other")'. Cordelia's experience underlines the point.

> It does change when you get more senior because people are then completely stunned and shocked, and really, you know, they don't know how to deal with it at all. They can't quite believe that you are the boss. There were lots of times I turned up for meetings with other members of staff and people would find it really difficult. They would keep talking to my [white] member of staff. They found it really hard to accept that I was the decision-maker and I was going to be giving them the money.
>
> (Cordelia)

Another participant described the way she was sometimes implicitly demoted by the head of the cultural institution where she worked, an act that made her less visible, 'placed' her more appropriately in the archetypal institutional hierarchy that whiteness dictates (in this particular case, one marked by class and gender as well as race) and, correspondingly, made her presence easier to accept. In relating the story, however, she provided evidence that showed the demotion to be completely unjustified, and instead revealed the illogical sub-jectivity that whiteness normalizes: 'The interesting thing is I am the head of a department, I've got a team, I've got a budget and you know, the president and his wife sometimes introduce me, "Meet Shoma, ((whispers)) she's our press officer"' (Shoma, focus group 5). The desire to put and keep the 'other' in her place – particularly in social contexts where 'respectability' matters – is reminiscent of colonial concerns about the dangers posed by an uncontrollable, irrational other, who may disturb the smooth running of Empire unless properly contained. In the modern occupational context, 'containing' the 'other' equates to curtailing their status by refusing to recognize and publicly acknowledge their skills and leadership.

Using liminal knowledge to contest merit and client

Participants frequently drew on their liminal experience and knowledge to enhance their 'reading' of racialization in PR, explicitly commenting on what their colleagues might be thinking, the grounds for the judgements they made, and the reasons why they might find it difficult to accept a BAME practitioner on equal terms. As outsiders-within PR, with plentiful professional understanding and familiarity with a wide range of cultural and social capital, they had a bank of knowledge on which to draw for their interpretations of events.

Liminal knowledge came into its own when participants tried to make sense of the clearly biased application of merit to their careers, a process that they recog-nized as both gendered and classed. They contested the normative claim of 'objective' merit and instead argued that occupational rewards were offered based on subjective assessments of what type of person (rather than what type of work) deserved to be rewarded.

> [w]hite men were being paid more than white women, but white women were being paid more than me. So it was a sliding scale, it wasn't just about me, I would find. And, you know, white men would get the plum accounts, white women would get the next set of accounts and I would get the ones with clients that nobody wanted to look after.
>
> (Mavis, focus group 7)

Participants also knew that objective forms of merit were not measured in the same way for them as for their colleagues. On the contrary, their experiences showed that whiteness enhanced the objective achievements of typical colleagues, while it reduced the value of their own. As Katy put it in her diary: 'How can I compete against "I really like you?"' Participants knew their talent was less readily recognized, even to the point of making them almost invisible when it came to being rewarded.

> There were a number of times where I had meetings with HR. I said, 'I'm achieving my objectives, you've set me goals and I've achieved all of those yet I'm not seeing anything, I'm not moving forward'. And they just didn't give me proper reasoning, and they said it would happen, it would happen [...] and, you know, I was working really hard, like I was putting in 110% and I just felt like there were people that had come in after me that maybe, you know, were fulfilling their role but not exceeding it and they were getting further than I was.
>
> (Madhu)

Other participants challenged the normative role of the client as an implicit benchmark for assessments about identity and 'fit'. In contrast to the way in which occupational discourses engage almost single-mindedly with the pursuit of client homology to deliver occupational and organizational benefits, some participants shifted the focus of the argument to consider the negative effects of homology on individual practitioners. They argued that such a narrow view of 'fit' limited important career opportunities for practitioners who did not embody whiteness, regardless of their experience. For example, in the case of the following participant, his experience as a senior manager leading accounts for global brands in the African market, was apparently irrelevant to his ability to deliver appropriate service to clients in the United Kingdom.

> The thing is as a minority you've got two layers of challenges. First I'm black. You don't have a lot of black people in PR, right? One. Then secondly I'm African, with an African accent, with my substantial part of my career life coming from Africa and Africa is not seen as a very advanced market in PR. So … the agency would be reluctant to put me in front of a client and

say, 'This guy is going to be in charge of your account' because the client might feel, 'Okay well you're not resourcing my account with the right people'. I understood that, but it was a setback for me because if you are not in account management, you don't get to really understand what's going on in the market and I think that's a challenge, any other PR practitioner that is of a minority group and coming here to practice, that's one of the things they'll face because, for instance, in every agency I've worked in I've been the only black person. Then the only black African. The only African. So I'm just like a single person standing there, it's not a very good experience, but I've managed to scale through.

(Thomas)

Thomas' reflection is worth quoting at length because it illustrates the way he uses his liminal position as a senior professional who understands the importance of trust and homology to client relationships, and a Black man on whom racialized subjectivities are imposed, to see and articulate both sides of the 'argument' for and against putting him in client-facing roles. Strikingly, he role-plays the conversation that might take place between white senior manager and the client should he be given the account manager role. His business acumen allows him to understand (though perhaps not forgive) the rationale for excluding him, and, equally, recognize the importance of the denial of market knowledge – an indirect, but crucial negative side-effect of limited client-facing experience in PR. Ironically, it is precisely what whiteness denies him – his professional expertise – that enables him to accurately interpret his situation. In this particular case, however, his understanding offered him few options for resistance, other than a determination to continue his career despite the difficulty he faces.

Networking was potentially difficult for BAME practitioners, because they had to overcome white colleagues' unease before they could start building relationships. A further issue was white colleagues' relative ignorance of other cultures and ethnicities, which introduced the potential for BAME practitioners to be reduced to a spectacle, subjected to being looked-over as an essentialized object (rather than looked-past, or overlooked). For example, Anza, a British Asian and practising Muslim who wore a hijab, told of a PR awards dinner where her difference became more, rather than less visible as the night wore on, and colleagues assumed the right to comment on her 'abnormal' identity:

You can tell people are looking at you and talking about you. And then they feel the need to come over and say … 'So how do you find it? You must find it really difficult. *You know, you're not the normal person*'.

(Anza, focus group 3, emphasis added)

Here, a fascination with 'exotic' ethnicity devalues Anza's skills and achievements and eclipses the fact that she is attending the dinner as a fellow professional. Related forms of 'othering' were grounded in assumptions among white practitioners that their BAME colleagues lived in a social and cultural world that had no correspondence to their own and, therefore, that they would have little in common. Again, the participants' liminal perspective of whiteness in PR and understanding of the stereotypes associated with their race and class, meant that they could follow colleagues' assumptions about what kinds of cultural or social capital they may or may not have in common. In the following example, Cordelia does not role play an explicit conversation about her identity in the way Thomas does, but instead articulates the internal voices of white practitioners, revealing the prejudices, fear and uncertainty that emerge when the 'other' comes too close.

> [T]here is just that, 'We're not used to dealing with those sorts of people', or 'Those sorts of people are only fit for certain situations'. So, 'I only meet those people when I'm on the tube, or when one of them's trying to steal my bag', or, you know, so '...to have them sitting round a board table on equal terms I just ... it's outside of my reality and I don't know how to treat them, I don't know how to behave'. [...] [They] assume that I won't have had any of the experiences or the background that they've had. And then they think, 'Well, you know, she won't have gone skiing over Easter, or she won't have popped down to Prada to buy a new ... so what are we going to talk about? She won't have been to the theatre, you know, and maybe we're going to have to talk about the MOBOs or we're going to have to talk about jerk chicken...
>
> (Cordelia)

Assumptions, of course, are not grounded in experience; once again, the critique of whiteness revolves around its disconnection from other lives (the implication is that white colleagues would not be comfortable talking about the MOBOs or jerk chicken), and its focus on difference rather than similarity (BAME practitioners are assumed not to engage with the same types of (elite) leisure and culture). As a heretical presence, then, the 'other' destabilizes the apparent self-confidence of whiteness; in a world that otherwise requires relatively little effort from white colleagues, they are suddenly required to think about how they should behave – and are faced with the reality that they 'don't know'. Such ignorance, of course, is not something that marginalized practitioners suffer from, since they are required to pass between the spaces marked by whiteness and 'other' identities on a daily basis. Once again, whiteness is revealed as deficient, even as it seems to be hegemonic.

Conclusion: heresy, identity and resistance

The field of PR, constructed through the eyes of the 'other', throws into relief the static, fixed nature of the occupational doxa and its archetypes. Re-constructing the occupational field from a heretical perspective reveals how the field itself is defined and limited by racialization; it loses fluidity, flexibility and the ability to engage with and respond to the world it claims to know. It is the 'other' who introduces flexibility, challenges meanings, representations, identities and points out where they are inaccurate, misguided or simply wrong.

Thus, participants in the study reflected on and challenged PR's occupational doxa and habitus by deconstructing the whiteness that marked its discourses and practices, revealing the fictional nature of its claims to universality and objectivity, and making visible the political conditions of its existence. In so doing, they introduced a different perspective of PR as an occupation deeply concerned with power: the power to preserve and extend its legitimacy. Their narratives illustrated how this power frequently operated at occupational and organizational level, in informal interactions with colleagues and during formal processes, by imposing subjectivities on them that had more to do with historical stereotypes than their professional skills. Their reconstruction of the field from the standpoint of the 'other' incorporated, rather than masked, the flaws in discourse and practice that blind adherence to whiteness produced. Their perspective reintroduced issues of occupational and organizational power and broadened discourse from focusing solely on clients, organizations and markets, to incorporate the moral and ethical effects of PR in both their own lives and the lives of the audiences targeted by PR work.

Understanding the field 'warts and all', created space for them to talk about, rationalize and begin to combat the fundamentally inequitable effects it had on their own working lives. But it also came with risks: such a fundamental re-writing of the occupational field equates to a form of 'heretical discourse' (Bourdieu, 2000), because it questions the very foundation of PR's occupational identity and the grounds for the apparent superiority of white, middle-class practitioners. The heresy in question is to claim that white dominance in PR is accidental, rather than merit-based, and that it is sustained through gendered and classed processes of racialization, normalized through the occupational habitus. For those who exercise this critique – whether as an explicit challenge, or merely by their presence – the risk of further marginalization or even exclusion becomes a reality. For practitioners who want a successful career, the wise option is frequently to limit their agency and resistance to the context of their own career, without challenging the systemic nature of the racialization they see and experience. As a result, the integrity of the occupational field survives unscathed, and the impetus for diversity initiatives to generate change that goes beyond individual cases is significantly weakened. In the next chapter, I explore the ways these dynamics are reflected in concrete strategies that participants used to tackle whiteness, based on their nuanced reading of the complexities in their occupational and organizational environments.

6 Successful marginality
Managing occupational identity

The heretical occupational field that practitioners constructed not only gave them space to articulate their experiences, but also provided information about the implicit aspects of their environment that they had to navigate in order to achieve success. In other words, for marginalized practitioners, it was not only the formally articulated occupational archetype that provided resources for developing a powerful professional identity, but also the heretical 'other' occupation that they experienced on a day-to-day basis. The former provided information about what they were supposed to be and do as if they were any other professional; the latter gave them guidance about how their embodiment of these archetypes would be seen differently as a result of the implicit subjectivities attributed to them. The institutional and experiential dimensions of intersectionality informed its intersubjective and organizational manifestations, enabling practitioners to develop strategies for 'successful marginality' that would enable them to manage their workplace identity *in the context of others' reactions to it* (Hurtado, 1996). As one participant put it, 'you have to juggle, you have to show something that will let them maybe not look at [ethnicity] so much' (Sharon).

Successful marginality, then, was a means for participants to maximize control over the way their identity was constructed, renegotiating their position in different encounters over time. Their approach to identity as a 'temporary attachment to subject positions' (Hall, 1996: 4) gave them the flexibility to respond to racialization in ways that were most productive for their own occupational interests. They took advantage of the fact that their identities could never be completely fixed, that 'ultimately, meaning begins to slip and slide; it begins to drift, or be wrenched or inflected into new directions' (Hall, 2013: 259). Such flexibility was crucial since racialization re-emerged time and again in different forms and different situations; the risk of marginalization – and the need to manage it – was constant. Reflecting the fact that racialization is a systemic process, participants' narratives reflected the continual need to manage identity carefully in that they did not speak in terms of individual, isolated episodes of racism, but more in terms of patterns of discrimination that they had had to tackle throughout their careers. Even when practitioners could draw successfully on a range of professional, cultural and social capital to manage their identity, the risk of racialization never completely disappeared.

The condensed subjectivities that accompanied their arrival into each new situation, as stereotypes they had to confront and deflect, meant that their claims to insider status were never secure and placed an added burden on them, which their white colleagues never had to face. Perhaps the most dramatic example of this was given by one practitioner who told of her experience accompanying a senior colleague on a prison visit relatively early in her career. Her racial identity and assumptions about her class meant that she embodied the *potential* for criminality in the spaces where she worked, latent until it was called forth as an appropriate categorization, at which point it overrode her professional status.

> We were chatting away and then one of the inmates shouts out 'Oy! Cordelia! Hello.' And I thought 'Oh my god it's my worst nightmare, I'm trying to impress. Don't tell me, you know, it's some old school friend. Oh what a nightmare.' So I ignored it. And anyway, he didn't stop, he shouted again. And so James, the Director said, 'Oh, look, it's one of your relatives'. It was awful, an absolutely awful moment.
>
> (Cordelia)

Identity does not transfer across situations, as Hall notes, but is constructed anew each time, under different conditions and without a guaranteed outcome. For the participants in the study, their identity in novel environments was almost always the 'space invader' (Puwar, 2004), whose right to belong was open to question. In the preceding example, Cordelia was on the 'wrong' side of the prison bars, in the eyes of her director; consequently, her presence was not secure. His racist assumption that her family was criminal, even if she wasn't, allowed him to undermine her professional status and place her, by association, in the space where her presence would no longer threaten his dominance.

Similar experiences of 'othering' were shared by many other participants, from a Polish practitioner whose colleagues assumed she was receiving some welfare benefits even while she was working full time, to the implicit assumption that Black practitioners were working-class rather than middle-class, and the stereotypes of Black women as 'sexy, they're exotic, they have tons of kids by different men so they're quite sexual' (Terrie), echoing the characters of both 'Sapphire' (difficult, argumentative and not appropriately feminine) and Jezebel (insatiably promiscuous) that have marked representations of Black women (Ladson-Billings, 2009; bell hooks, 1994). Thus, even though participants may be invested with formal authority, their professional status is permanently at risk of being sidelined by the stereotypes that come into play when her behaviour is interpreted and their performance assessed.

Despite the regularity of being racialized, participants were repeatedly surprised to encounter racism. Again and again, their narratives revealed the ways in which the identities that whiteness attributed to them were not internalized, but (re)discovered, fought against or rejected. They 'discovered [their] blackness, [their] ethnic characteristics' (Fanon, 2008(1952): 84). As one diarist put it:

When I find myself in such a situation, it often makes me realize that I am more Asian to others than I am to myself! I rarely speak anything other than English, rarely eat anything other than British or European food, I watch English or American films, same with musical tastes and so, am actually not very Asian at all!!

(Ivor, diary)

There was also repeated disappointment and frustration at the prejudice they encountered, not least because of the repetitive and formulaic form it took – for example, as 'inevitable' questions about background or country of origin, or the regular overlooking of professional skills and achievements: 'All these things were on my CV when I was first recruited. Nevertheless, I have to prove myself again and again. That's very tiring and disheartening.' (Aaron, diary). Sometimes, experiences were more painful and racism more overt; one diarist's religious observance was described by a colleague – who was otherwise supportive of his religious needs – as him doing his 'Jew shit' and 'bunking off' on a Friday (when he left early to observe the Jewish Sabbath).

In the remainder of this chapter, I illustrate how participants adopted a range of strategies to manage their identity in the face of racialization. Sometimes the focus was on 'acting white', contradicting stereotypes about their race and/or class. At other times, they turned the 'grit' their race represented into 'grease'. They used their intersectionality strategically, drawing on different forms of capital to demonstrate their fit, and they attempted to demonstrate the personal characteristics of 'fit' (creativity, confidence, sociability) that the normative PR habitus prescribes. In all cases, the desired outcome was to encourage colleagues and institutions to orient towards, rather than away from them (Ahmed, 2006). However, as I will describe, the effects of their strategies were not always straightforward; they were more or less successful, and always tinged with the knowledge that the struggle to fit in was ongoing, since racialization itself refused to disappear.

Successful marginality in practice

Participants chose a range of things to 'juggle' as part of their identity management, most frequently in ways that minimized the salience and visibility of their racial and/or class identity. Very common were strategies that focused colleagues on their professional skills, particularly the quality and volume of their work, rather than on their race. Participants frequently worked long hours to complete tasks to a high standard, reversing stereotypes that they lacked skill, intellect or were unreliable (Hall, 2013), and reframing the reference points for their embodiment from race to commitment and collegiality, forms of subjective merit that permeated the occupational field (see Chapter 4).

I was very enthusiastic and I used to work extra hard and all the rest of it, and so bosses always like that and they forget your colour after a while because they just think, 'Well, if you want it done, ask Cordelia and she'll do it,' and that's what worked for me in the end.

(Cordelia)

Participants not only worked long and hard, but frequently tried to exceed expectations in the ways they carried out their roles. Going beyond the call of duty again echoed the ideas of commitment and passion privileged in occupational discourses but it also functioned as a form of racial comforting (Carbado and Gulati, 2013) in that it helped colleagues feel at ease around the participants' presence and reduced the degree to which they were seen to be 'out of place' (Puwar, 2004).

So I thought the other way for me to prove myself is to make sure if somebody's on a call or talking I quickly try and pick up their phone and then try and react myself and, you know, answer the query and then follow up as well 'Is there anything else you need, a case study or...' you know, just try and really build my name and make sure they're aware that I'm there, I'm not in the background of the press office.

(Anza)

The effects of identity management strategies were complex. Sometimes, working harder, longer and more enthusiastically did deliver the advantage of making the marginalized practitioner visible in an environment where, they knew, they were liable to being overlooked. It countered instinctive institutional or collegial orientation away from them and instead bolstered their visibility as an insider, rather than an outsider-within. As the preceding quote suggests, visibility was linked to reputation; you cannot have a reputation if you are 'in the background'. Ironically, sometimes exceeding expectations and developing a reputation was easier because of the low expectations that colleagues had:

It's also an advantage because when ... when they have such low expectations and then they see me and maybe they see my output they go, 'Wow this is really good. This report is really good. This proposal is really good.' So, I mean, whenever I'm given the opportunity it makes me feel good that, okay yes I'm beginning to prove myself and that has happened over and over again.

(Thomas)

Demonstrating professional capability, then, was a way of modifying the 'grit' that race represented into 'grease', where work habits and commitment were pushed to the foreground. The racial comforting it generated, however, was never complete in that new challenges reintroduced the 'baggage' of old subjectivities and stereotypes that implicitly told participants to 'stay within bounds, to go back where [they] belonged' (Fanon, 2008[1952]: 86). Thus, Thomas has to prove 'over and over again' that he is able to participate fully as a professional, capable of strategic insight and analysis. Consequently, strategies of working harder to combat racialization came with a long-term risk of burnout, precisely because merit is not measured equitably across the occupational field, and BAME practitioners must do more, *repeatedly*, to be recognized. 'I've always just worked extra, extra hard. Which isn't always the answer actually. It's very unfair because you just end up physically done in' (Cordelia).

The subjective nature of merit also meant that working harder and longer could result in no change to the participants' position; having constructed the evidence that they deserve the same reward as their colleagues, they found that their potential victory over discrimination disappeared because their racialized identity altered the terms of engagement (Fanon, 2008). Such situations resulted in practitioners questioning their strategy. One participant described in her diary the way she 'felt like a mug for working so hard' after discovering that other colleagues had been given a discretionary promotion while she had been ignored (Katy, diary). At the same time, being visible sometimes led to participants becoming hyper-visible. The scrutiny that followed could be uncomfortable and undermine confidence.

> When my colleagues speak, there's an interaction between them and the client. When I speak, there's silence and everyone is focusing on me. I think it's because they are trying to support me but actually their effort has the opposite effect and makes me lose confidence in myself. […] I understand that my accent can be difficult to understand but not that difficult that you have to focus hard and be silent … and I had a meeting that went much better with another client the same week, that's why I could really feel the difference.
>
> (Amy)

The higher risks associated with making mistakes meant that some participants felt they were more cautious than they might otherwise have been in going about their work, producing 'an over-focus on process which I think can suffocate work and creativity' (Sharon, focus group 5). This particular racial double-bind is particularly problematic for BAME PR practitioners, given that the archetypal practitioner identity demands creativity, passion and a willingness to 'go the extra mile' in efforts to deliver a unique solution for client needs. Standing out from the crowd signifies suitability and fit with the field's requirements, but is more complicated for BAME PR practitioners to realize, precisely because being visible carries the risk of inviting scrutiny and producing marginalization should unusual, stand-out activities go wrong.

The disadvantage of hyper-visibility notwithstanding, there were occasions when it led to opportunities that participants could take advantage of, recognizing and exploiting the strategic value they offered to their employers as examples of 'happy diversity' (Ahmed, 2009), the embodiment of institutional diversity and a means of constructing better relations with 'other' audiences. In the following quote, the participant recognizes the value of her international upbringing to her colleagues, and the commercial value that her complex ethnic heritage provides:

[M]y bio is a selling point that I lived in ten cities. [...] I've been the lead on some global [brand] business lately and I think a lot of that is because I, I'm very comfortable in New York, I'm very comfortable in London. I have an Indian background – I basically represent six of their foreign markets. So I think if anything it's been to my advantage. [...] I've had nothing but positive feedback about my ethnicity and I, I feel like it's given me more edge.

(Aisha)

Participants who did not have the same elite international heritage found other ways to make their race 'matter' in ways that would benefit, rather than disadvantage them, including taking opportunities that were offered to them on the basis of their ethnicity, perhaps before their professional acumen. This was a particularly useful strategy if there was an instance of interest convergence (Bell, 1980), where, for example, a client or employer wanted to reach a particular ethnic minority community. In such cases, practitioners were able to re-cast their difference as occupational merit, echoing the rationale for diversity that dominates business discourse: 'I think it's been quite beneficial to be a part of a team that's not necessarily got that many ethnic minorities within it, because it brings in a different perspective and it can help' (Aaron). As one diarist noted, however, this form of interest convergence did not *displace* stereotypes; on the contrary, it was always grounded in some kind of stereotypical assumption about race or ethnicity.

Called in by local authority to support them during a meeting with CEO and marketing chap from an international bank, which has its HQ in India. To be honest, I was asked to attend because of my ethnicity – as an Asian professional, there was a gross assumption made that I was an expert on the make-up of the Asian business community in the city. I guess it was an example of 'positive' discrimination, if it is possible for discrimination to be positive. Did I mind? I guess not, as the intentions were sound and I guess it was a privilege to be invited to support senior officials of the local authority at such a high level meeting. I was invited 1. because I am Asian 2. because I am a businessman and 3. the local authority felt I could add value to their presentation – there's not really anything wrong with this.

(Ivor, diary)

Race, in these situations, becomes commodified as a communicative advantage; race-as-diversity has value that can be realized for the organization, providing occasions where practitioners can promote their skills. In the process, however, race is emptied of its complex association with identity; 'valued' diversity is inflexible and separated from the individual who is 'diverse', insofar as it has to be embodied in a way that meets the organization's needs (Ahmed, 2009). Participants often expressed uncertainty and ambivalence about taking up such opportunities, as illustrated by the repeatedly hesitant 'I guess', 'to be honest', 'there's not really anything wrong' in Edward's diary excerpt. While the opportunities were recognized as personally valuable, they were grounded in a system that did not usually support BAME practitioners or their ambitions.

> I know my value is, sometimes I have to face audiences that somebody else, it wouldn't be appropriate, not appropriate but it wouldn't go down as well. For example, the one bit of TV I've managed to do for here was, we had a [crisis] in Brixton and then BBC London asked to do a piece at one of the sites [...] My colleague covers it, he's a white male, but he is part Jewish, so if you want the diversity it's there, but they said no. [...] And it's in Brixton. They said 'We want you to do it'. I hadn't had any media training and I'm like, why? And then it kind of clicked and I went 'Oh, okay. (laughs) Okay, I'll go'. I'll just feel the fear and do it anyway. And I was kind of like, well actually why not? I mean no one out in their press office is from an ethnic minority.
>
> (Terrie)

In this situation, Terrie's Jewish colleague was not appropriate, while she had the advantage of being both Black (which fitted the audience demographic) and middle-class (which meant she was acceptable as a spokesperson for the company). Language played an important role because it was an immediate and highly visible aspect of identity that she knew could be used as an indicator of class and educational background that facilitated strategic passing: 'It's okay for me sat here, my parents paid for elocution, I've got a quite good sounding voice, I'm reasonably well presented, so most people can sort of allow a glaze of colour-blindness'. As her comment suggests, the mix of cultural capital she was able to claim meant that people could choose when they wanted to recognize her race and when to ignore it, creating a fluidity around her identity that she could exploit. However, Terrie's story also highlights the limitations of interest convergence as a source of long-term change, since it makes race an optional element of identity, drawn on when the value it represents is required, rather than being fully accepted.

The TV appearance was a positive professional opportunity for her personally, but also reflected the importance that many practitioners placed on their role as someone who could educate organizations and the occupation more widely about diverse audiences, combating stereotypes that ignored the differences between, for example, Chinese, Korean and Japanese identities (Anna, diary), or the varied sub-groupings within Asian and Black communities (Ivor, diary).

Some participants adopted the strategy of exploiting stereotypes (Carbado and Gulati, 2013) as part of their occupational identity management, either recognizing their backgrounds as a source of unique, unusual attraction, or taking advantage of opportunities grounded in their 'other' ethnicity. They knew the fact that they didn't look like the occupational norm was an advantage, and may even prompt preconceptions of a higher level of skill. For the following participant, the stereo-typical identity of Indian male professionals lent his presence more gravitas:

> [B]ecause I was working in the technology sector and working predomi-nantly on business campaigns I think as a guy walking into a room and meeting a marketing director or a CEO and sitting down and saying, 'This is what I think,' and being as far away from a blond-haired airhead as is possible to be, I think that's definitely helped because it's kind of … it's not what they expect and I probably look like their accountant or their lawyer.
>
> (Edward)

The limited understanding of different ethnicities among white colleagues led some participants to try to familiarize colleagues with aspects of their culture, hoping to ameliorate the ignorance that caused uncertainty and friction around them. Food, traditional dress, or music were introduced as non-political, safe aspects of their identity simultaneously communicating that the practitioners themselves were not a 'dangerous' presence in the field. As the following quote shows, the limits to what colleagues would find acceptable (the 'good stuff') were fairly clear:

> I try and bring the good stuff into the office … like at Jewish festivals I bring in the relevant food, so it might be cheesecake or it might be kind of biscuits or whatever, so I try and make it fun and interesting for them. I don't how-ever, for example, when I'm out on a Friday say, 'I'm out of office because it's the Jewish Sabbath and here's a link to Wikipedia on Shabbat'.
>
> (Aaron, diary)

Such educational strategies, however, were also frustrating. The same participant, in a diary entry about leaving his current workplace for a new job, reflected on the double-edged sword of making ethnicity 'safe' to discuss in the workplace, but only at a very shallow level. Being limited to showing the 'good stuff' meant in-depth discussion of his Jewish heritage and identity rarely emerged. The hesi-tation in the way he expresses his feelings about the situation reflects the difficulty of breaking out of liminal space in that genuine changes in attitude require the surfacing of deeper stereotypes and imaginaries than can be achieved by just showing the 'good stuff'. By definition, the 'good stuff' is the stuff that does not threaten, does not raise the spectre of power being displaced, and is therefore only a weak tool for educating white colleagues about the 'other'. Stereotypes, both fantastical and overt, are likely to prevail (Hall, 2013: 252).

> One of the administrators said of my leaving 'No more Jewish cakes!'. I tried to work out whether I felt happy or sad about that. It's nice that someone felt a connection in that way I suppose – and that I had a quasi-educational impact, but was my attempt at celebration and education being considered as nothing more than a feeding frenzy? I hope not. I did it because I feel it's

important to share, demystify, celebrate one's identity [...] I think it helps people understand who I am and means I will get less suspicion/uncertainty/ anxiety from people when they want to talk to me. However, I'd like to think I'm really giving them something to take away other than ... cake ...

(Aaron, diary)

While the aforementioned strategies focused on managing the ways in which meaning and value was attached to race and ethnicity, participants also leveraged their knowledge of the occupational habitus to access some of the 'grease' that white colleagues seemed to enjoy. Social capital was one key resource that was relatively easy to acquire. Participants networked strategically to build professional reputation across the occupational field: 'You have to just try and network ruthlessly and try and work harder and get known for, you know, for doing a good job in projects' (Nila). Seeking out mentors was another more targeted means of developing social capital, particularly useful within organizations as an important way of overcoming their 'outsider-within' status, by ensuring access to know-how about institutional politics and strategies, and having insiders support their claim to belong in the field.

[Mentoring is] extremely important whatever colour you are in any, in any career, but much more so in an area where you don't see anyone like yourself, and you [...] want to make sure you're not out of the loop because you might be excluded in some way. So you need that, someone who's got good inside information, good experience and can give you good direction and advice.

(Kathy, focus group 5)

Strategic intersectionality (Fraga *et al.*, 2006) describes the ways in which individuals draw on sources of subjectivity that provide ways of offsetting disadvantage, and some participants spoke of the normative social and cultural capital from their class background that had facilitated their entry and progress in PR. Assets they drew on included a degree from a top-ranked university; family connections; and access to elite social and political networks. Edward explicitly recognized the ways in which such capital helped him demonstrate the kind of personality that gave him a competitive edge when interviewing for his first job – a 'sparky' intellect.

I remember during the interview she didn't really care about what university I went to, what got her excited was my being an editor of a student newspaper and that whole journalistic process [...] I think that's what counted with her. I think with Michael the fact that I'd gone to Oxford was a kind of reassurance I think because [...] he was kind of looking at more broader, 'does this fit my criteria of bright and sparky individuals that I want to be working at my agency with?'

(Edward)

Edward's student media career had helped him access the 'critical frameworks of meaning' (Anderson-Gough *et al.*, 2006: 252) that shaped the media environment, through valuable engagement with important media networks (he had developed connections with national media during his time as the editor of the Oxford University student newspaper). Consequently, he could demonstrate knowledge of 'that whole journalistic process' in the interview, in a way that competitors couldn't. Similarly, the following quote shows how Aadi's family history of engagement in local politics gave him networks in and knowledge about the political environment, crucial social and cultural capital that opened doors for him as he moved into a communications career.

> And so [my parents] had an interest in politics, so [...] to get involved locally and understand the local decision-making [...], the political Labour Party was easy in that that door was open effectively. [T]hen at university political society becomes very accessible anyway. And when it came to getting the job in Parliament, I guess, which was my first career in, in communication, the wider communication industry and the party political industry, I think it helped, the fact that I'd run for Parliament.
>
> (Aadi)

As these examples suggest, participants clearly recognized the importance of subjective aspects of 'fit' that mark the archetypal practitioner identity, including confidence, commitment and sociability. As well as demonstrating work habits and networks that exemplified these characteristics, some participants focused on strategically managing their physical presence in ways that could deflect any focus on their race: 'whether it's in an interview or a boardroom setting you have to dazzle by your confidence so it overcomes anything they may be thinking subconsciously, you know, it just pushes it away' (Anjali, focus group 2). The process was not always undertaken willingly, but it was recognized as a necessity if one was to create the 'right' impression.

> There are times that, you know, you have to change the way you are and, and dress appropriately when you're going to a certain meeting and show an image which may not be true to you but you have to portray it just to pander to other people's needs.
>
> (Nila)

Many participants talked about their efforts to assimilate new forms of cultural knowledge as part of a strategy to develop the cultural omnivorousness (Peterson and Kern, 1996) that would allow them to socialize and mix comfortably with a wide range of people, as required by the occupational archetype.

> I thought, it's not really something that really interests me – do I want to spend £65 on getting a ticket to go and see, you know, the ballet or going to the theatre up in the West End? But because people at work were doing

it in PR and then talking about it with journalists, I started to, with no interest other than it might help me, I can fit in with conversations that are
happening.

(Anza)

However, some cultural capital could never be accessed, as those participants
who had not grown up in Britain realized. Their lack of familiarity with historical
forms of British popular culture was a major factor in their exclusion from social
and work-related interactions. As one practitioner noted in her diary, expectations
that she would 'chip in' to a chat between her client and a journalist were impossible to meet because she had not grown up in Britain and did not share their
reference points.

It made me feel kind of excluded and showed me that no matter how much
I read, watch, participate in British culture etc., I'll never acquire certain
knowledge. Certain things are closed to me. [...] So basically I dread the
question: 'And what do you think about this Amy?'

(Amy, diary)

For Amy, partial inclusion was achieved by keeping up with current popular
culture – but even this strategy was personally dissatisfying, since it required her
to spend extra time and effort watching programmes (mainly reality TV shows)
that didn't align with her own sense of identity and ethics.

There's not much I can do about gaining this 'old' knowledge that everyone
else is are familiar with, beside keeping up to date with what is happening
now and watching all TV shows! Really exhausting and I'm not really
proud of some of the TV shows I watch, but I feel I have to do this to know
what others are talking about.

(Amy, diary)

As Amy's comments illustrate, managing racialized workplace identities is hard
work and does not come without a cost (Carbado and Gulati, 2013). Physically,
practitioners widely recognized that working harder than other colleagues, while an
effective way of demonstrating some of the archetypal characteristics that the occupation required and proving one's worth, had a detrimental effect on their personal
lives and meant they were vulnerable to burn out. While long hours are not unusual
in PR (CIPR, 2011a), the additional symbolic meaning of such work habits for
marginalized practitioners means that choosing to opt out of the work culture is a
more difficult decision because it comes at a heavier cost: that of reinforcing the
stereotype that they are lazy, lack discipline or commitment, or that their loyalty lies
with the domestic sphere, rather than the professional world.

Psychologically, making efforts to ensure white practitioners feel at ease about
their presence, may require practitioners to deny important aspects of their identity
(Carbado and Gulati, 2013), a difficult task in itself, or to engage with activities that

they don't enjoy, as Amy's experience illustrates. The need to 'fit' resulted in them taking themselves 'far off from [their] own presence, far indeed, and [making themselves] an object' (Fanon, 2008[1952]: 85). Indeed, Fanon's description of this object-making as an amputation of identity was directly echoed by one participant, who tried to express the visceral importance of racial and ethnic identity: 'Human interaction requires you interact as a whole being, you can't sort of slice off one bit of who you are and engage, there's always going to be a disconnect' (Terrie).

The apparently endless need to monitor and manage identity in the face of permanent vulnerability to discrimination had an inevitable impact on BAME practitioners' confidence. Participants spoke about how it was difficult for BAME practitioners to 'bounce back' from crises where they may have made mistakes, whereas white colleagues found it much easier because their fundamental right to belong was not questioned.

> [I]n people's careers sometimes you may have [...] a Waterloo moment where everything just goes wrong, you know, around you. You might have a bad mistake or something awful will happen and black people find it hard to bounce back from that and often they may just disappear, you know, whereas those who are not black can bounce back and [...] they're even higher than they were before whereas for most of us it's harder to pull back up that ladder once you've had that moment.
>
> (Jane, focus group 5)

Some participants 'opted out' of particular situations as a means of self-protection. As Mavis explained, in the context of an organization where discrimination was both gendered and raced, she had been given the most difficult clients and expected to work for the least pay. In the end, and despite having turned the situation to her advantage, she moved away.

> Those difficult clients are people I know to this day and they've become part of my network, so I regarded that as a positive, but I did feel it was important to step away from that sort of experience because I think I could have still been in a company like that.
>
> (Mavis, focus group 7)

In contrast, the question of whether participants had been rewarded because of their ethnicity, rather than their professional skills, also had the potential to undermine practitioners' self-belief.

> I always do sometimes think, 'Am I, you know, getting this position, getting this job, am I being put forward for this because of my background?' The fact that I'm an ethnic minority. Does it ... you know, sometimes ... you know, it's just that little voice sometimes that says ... but I think I've ... I don't pay much attention to that.
>
> (Fahad)

Nonetheless, and reflecting a desire to identify and be recognized as a professional first and foremost, some practitioners reacted to discrimination with even greater determination to comply with the occupational 'game' and do well. As Andy points out, complicity in this case was not capitulation, but an active choice to resist stereotypes and prove others wrong: 'I don't think I'll let [the racist industry] stop me. [...] This focus on barriers could hold BME people back, and I just have to apply for things' (Andy, diary).

Conclusion: the limits of resistance?

Choosing the right strategy to combat racialization was clearly complicated, political and personal. The act of strategizing in itself challenged the implicit understanding of the 'other' that was represented by what occupational discourses did *not* say about who and what PR practitioners might be. Occupational 'othering' was overturned by participants' demonstrations of belonging that gave the lie to the superiority of whiteness in which PR's occupational project was grounded. In this sense, their strategies reflect Becker's (Becker *et al.*, 2009 [1961]) argument that it is not the occupation itself that defines who a professional is or can be, but the interactions of individuals with the occupation.

The *need* to demonstrate belonging was a result of the construction of difference-as-inferiority in occupational discourse, but its *enactment* was a way of reconstructing difference-as-distance. Participants did not pretend that they were not different from the norm, they did not want to be white, they did not accept the constructed inferiority imposed upon them, and they did not wish to reverse the relationship so that they were superior in the field and white practitioners inferior. On the contrary, in challenging prejudice they attempted to *disconnect difference from power* by addressing prejudice 'through the eye of representation' (Hall, 2013: 263), bridging the gap that PR's discourses construct between insiders and outsiders within the field, and demonstrating their own humanity, their wholeness rather than the partial identity that stereotyping imposed upon them (Fanon, 2008(1952)). Nonetheless, while they did not seek superiority, their actions prompted a redistribution of power in the field; as Bourdieu (1992) notes, the relational nature of fields means that if one party moves, others must move too. In asserting their belonging, participants did create space to act as and claim the identity of a PR professional, and white colleagues did make space for them in organizations and in the field. In terms of the micro-processes of power, then, they were successful.

One strategy that participants did not mention, however, was to challenge the field's racializing tendencies directly in their day-to-day work. They recognized that to overtly contest or question whiteness on the basis of its exclusionary effects would not facilitate progress. Rather, it would draw attention to the individual as a 'different' body, a body 'out of place' (Puwar, 2004): 'all you're doing is showing that you're different and that you don't fit in that kind of culture' (Mary, focus group 2). While participants understood how and why they were perceived in particular ways, their strategies of resistance were focused on specific events rather than the system itself. They never suggested, for example, that colleagues should be more reflective and reflexive about their *own* identity in the field. Indeed, to appeal to whiteness to inspect itself is a somewhat futile exercise: one reason whiteness survives is precisely because it appears natural to its inhabitants. To argue that it is not is a political challenge, not simply a point of order. It denies the myth of merit and colour-blindness, which leads inevitably to questions about the rights of insiders to their privileged position. Initiating such a challenge is a particularly risky business for those hoping to benefit from it.

The strategies discussed in this chapter show how participants recognized that success in PR depends on finding a way to become insiders by adopting, to a certain level at least, the 'illusio' that the field's habitus demands, by playing the occupational 'game' (Bourdieu, 2000). They have to invest in the corporate professionalization project, the pursuit of status and legitimacy for PR, and this means recognizing whiteness in the occupational doxa and habitus as the norm, even if they contest its validity in their own careers. They must demonstrate those aspects of whiteness that are available to them (for example, on the basis of their class and cultural or social capital) while minimizing the salience of their race. Alternatively, they have to construct their own racial identity with whiteness in mind, demonstrating that they do not present a threat, but rather that their racial identity is innocuous, 'good stuff'. Finally, they must demonstrate their commitment to the occupation by adjusting their work and leisure habits in ways that serve PR's interests.

All of these strategies are easier for those who can draw on privileged forms of capital for their workplace identity; indeed, where participants had attended elite schools, enjoyed links with politics and the media, or could demonstrate creativity and cultural omnivorousness, their racial identity was sometimes irrelevant to their experience. As 'familiar rather than unfamiliar strangers' in the field, they were at ease, and put others at ease around them (Puwar, 2004: 128). In the context of PR's corporate professionalization project, it meant they could be trusted to look after the interests of the occupation by responding positively to the disciplinary discourses of practice, knowledge, client and merit, adopting occupational norms and thereby reinforcing the validity of the occupation's jurisdiction (Hodgson, 2002; Abbott, 1988). At an organizational level, the ability to put other colleagues and institutions 'at ease' meant participants could be trusted to do the job of PR, and frequently (though not always) rewarded with responsibility and recognition. To all intents and purposes, they embodied a sufficient level of whiteness to make them a 'safe bet' (Carbado and Gulati, 2013). However, for those who came from a less privileged class background, who did not have access to the compensatory resources of appropriate social or cultural capital, the challenges of fitting in, being recognized and being rewarded, were more substantial.

As this chapter reveals, BAME practitioners adopted a reflexive approach to their careers, drawing on their liminal understanding of PR and their own intersectionality to understand and deal with the professional environment in ways that preserved their status within the field and minimized the racialization to which they were vulnerable. The dialectical interplay of institutional and individual power that results from these dynamics is the focus of Chapter 7, where I use Munshi and Edwards' approach (2011) to consider how this study can change the way we understand race, racialization and diversity in PR.

7 Occupational power, diversity and public relations

I argued in Chapter 1 that understanding diversity in PR is not a matter of simple numerical calculation, or of making PR workplaces more welcoming for new entrants. Diversity policies are, of course, welcome, and may lead to some positive interventions in individual workplaces. Participants did note good practices, including open and welcoming workplaces, being supported and encouraged by mentors and managers, a commitment to diversity from organizational leaders, and recruitment practices that included a strong focus on testing skills. Nonetheless, the danger of diversity initiatives remaining performative in and of themselves, rather than generating long term changes in voice and recognition for marginalized individuals, is great. In putting our trust in policy and good intentions, we run the risk of failing to recognize the fundamental dynamics of occupational self-interest that affect the fortunes of practitioners.

PR's corporate professionalization project, like all professionalization projects, is an exercise in self-preservation and advancement (Larson, 1977). It is undertaken by institutions and individuals, who must buy into it to make it work and ensure they can enjoy a successful career. It is also exclusionary, an effort to define who does and does not belong in PR, ostensibly justified on the basis of merit but in fact rooted in assumptions about the subjective characteristics of the kinds of people who are likely to support, rather than contradict, occupational narratives of identity and practice (Sommerlad, 2009; Bolton and Muzio, 2008). Understanding the nature of the professionalization project changes the way we understand the occupation and diversity within it. Professionalization, from this perspective, is not an objective set of practices, but 'is better understood as a claim, more or less successful in social confirmation' (Alvesson and Johansson, 2002: 243). Diversity initiatives must be understood in terms of the ways in which they reinforce or undermine such claims: do they facilitate a higher status for PR among those whose opinions lend it legitimacy and confirm its jurisdiction?

While PR could appeal to moral institutions for its legitimacy – the legal system, the political elite – in fact, PR's professionalization claims are an exercise in market-oriented justification (Boltanski and Thevenot, 2006[1991]). As an occupation whose growth has been tightly connected to the success of neoliberal economic and political philosophies, its disciplinary logic (Fournier, 1999) is grounded in an understanding of organizations as market mechanisms rather than social institutions, the state as a significant authority insofar as it facilitates markets, individualism and choice, and individuals as 'sovereign customers' (Du Gay *et al.*, 1994) whose needs must be understood and satisfied. The result is an occupation that justifies its legitimacy and jurisdiction on the basis of its ability to service clients and realize their interests through facilitating connection and dialogue with appropriate audiences. The moral case for PR and its potential to do good in society remain discursive sidelines, brought into play by industry associations as a means of deflecting critique rather than as a central pillar of the field's existence. As we saw in Chapters 3 and 4, the result is an occupation that is inherently biased towards a particular form of whiteness; a middle-class, white identity that fits easily with the market- and client-based imperatives of the field. Whiteness in PR does not question the fundamental supremacy of customer or organization; it caters to them.

The classed and racialized nature of PR is obscured by the archetypal status of whiteness, which universalizes its signifying power and enhances its disciplinary effect. Unlike other identities, it is expressly *not* located in particular situations, but can morph to fit whatever requirements dictate: 'as an "absent presence", [whiteness] seeks to stand for, and be a measure of, all humanity' (Sharma and Sharma, 2003: 306). It is underpinned by specific forms of cultural omnivorousness, intangible attributes such as passion, creativity and talent, and the ability to facilitate comfort and enthusiasm among those it engages. It is an identity that people orient towards and do not question; as such, it is eminently marketable, underpinning claims that PR itself can solve any problem for any organization. Whiteness, then, is essential to the survival and extension of the occupational project.

Understanding whiteness in this way reveals why located and historicized subjectivities, such as those attached to BAME practitioners, do not sit so easily within the field and might be understood as a threat to PR's professionalization project. They bring with them a reminder that the privilege of whiteness has never existed without its disadvantaged, discriminated 'other' against which it is defined. Rather than being universal and ephemeral, BAME practitioners must *come from somewhere*. To be located limits their utility to the occupation; it means they are more useful (marketable) in specific circumstances, rather than in general. They can be called on as required by external circumstances (for example, to embody diversity in a particular campaign, or to offer knowledge of a particular audience), but whiteness takes precedence elsewhere. And yet, their marked status as a minority within the field (made tangible in their everyday experience in organizations, at networking events, in meetings, among their colleagues) simultaneously *situates* the majority in their privileged position in the field, and raises uncomfortable questions about the origins of their power. Thus, the presence of BAME practitioners means that the universality of whiteness is challenged, the dominant narrative of whiteness as a naturally appropriate identity for PR is revealed as a fiction and the security it offers as a foundation for PR's strength and universal applicability becomes more fragile.

At the same time, however, the fact that BAME practitioners have chosen PR as a career, have bought into the doxa of the field, and understand the part they are expected to play in PR's occupational game, means they cannot be simply understood as victims of occupational dogma. On the contrary, their understanding of the professionalization project must be brought to bear on any analysis that purports to fully illustrate the dialectic of diversity in PR. They are not 'outsiders', although they may feel that way on occasion. They are outsiders-*within*, a liminal position that affords them significant power to manage the occupation's orientations towards them through various forms of workplace identity management (Carbado and Gulati, 2013). As Chapters 5 and 6 have shown, they contest and reinterpret PR's occupational narrative and bias towards whiteness in ways that reveal its flaws and inconsistencies. Their heretical discourse (Bourdieu, 1991), and the heretical field it constructs, gives them space to justify their presence and explain and manage their experience in ways that validate their identity as PR practitioners, rather than excuse their inclusion as an exception to the rule, or a means of realizing specific interests.

The reality of diversity in PR, then, is one of flux and change, struggle and counter-struggle over the ways recognition and value are accorded to the voices and, ultimately, the accounts given of PR by different members of the field. Returning to the broad questions I raised in the introduction, that have framed the empirical analysis, how might we summarize these dialectics?

Racialized elites/racialized non-elites

The focus in this book has been on how the history and current context of the PR industry leads to the discursive construction of elite archetypes of practice and practitioners that reflect the historical superiority of white subjectivities over their 'other' and support the neoliberal emphasis on markets, clients/consumers and choice at the expense of societal good. The archetypes are recognized as artifice by BAME practitioners, and are easily deconstructed through a liminal lens. However, for all their fragility, the racialized norms on which the archetypes stand have the potential to significantly affect practitioners' lives. Race is apparently irrelevant to the white, classed and gendered practitioners who enjoy a privileged position in the occupation; their inclusion in the field is grounded in seemingly objective forms of merit (elite education, track record, 'talent') and on 'natural' suitability (sociability, creativity, commitment). For BAME practitioners, in contrast, race is made relevant – an act that transforms it into a difference that matters – at moments when they become invisible, or less visible, than their colleagues despite their seniority or experience. It is made relevant when their authority is intentionally ignored, or when they are re-placed discursively into more junior positions. It is made relevant when their presence, or intellect, or professional skill is a matter of surprise and uncertainty rather than a matter of course; it is made relevant when it is commodified as part of the business rationale for their inclusion, a way to justify PR's contribution to diversity (or to communicating diversity) more effectively. In all these cases, the way race is used by the field and its insiders serves to shore up the elite status of insider practitioners by providing them with a foil against which they can reflect their 'superior' classed, gendered and racialized forms of whiteness.

However, it would be dangerous to over-emphasize the important of race in determining elite status. While my position in this book is that it has an effect on one's position in the occupational hierarchy that is irreducible to class, gender or other social categorizations, intersectionality shows that the latter can be used to change the way racialized subjectivities are managed, projected and received. BAME practitioners can and do use different forms of cultural and social capital associated with their class and professional status, to assert their legitimacy and authority in the occupational field. They also draw on their own liminal experience and family histories of life in the United Kingdom, as sources of capital that provide self-confidence and insight into how they are positioned and understood in the context of whiteness. Their resultant workplace and occupational identity management is enacted intersubjectively during daily interactions, as well as at organizational and institutional levels in formal meetings, during campaign activities, and in recruitment and promotion processes. It allows them to strategically 'pass' as normatively white (embodying or demonstrating certain required attributes of whiteness) and move between elite and non-elite areas of the occupational field as their career progresses.

Visible/invisible

The idea that race and ethnicity can be managed leads us to recognize that visibility of racialized identities is both fluid and relative; like race, visibility is located in time and place, and changes depending on context. At first glance, PR's legitimacy and jurisdiction obscures racialization, because it is explained in terms of the need for reputation management in a complex communicative environment, a strategy that places organizations and their interests at the centre of PR activities. As explained in Chapter 3, audiences for PR activity are framed primarily in organizational terms, and if they are only indirectly affected by the organization's actions, they are invisible in the occupational narrative. Consequently, the kind of knowledge that counts most in the field is that which relates to organizations, markets, and communication processes for audiences that matter.

The emphasis on professional knowledge leads inexorably to a parallel professional identity, framed by the language and habitus sanctioned in the field. Practitioners are described in terms that qualify them for their roles: as experts who demonstrate a track record of successful campaigns, can provide detailed knowledge of a particular market sector, or can access a network of media contacts and a black book of potential new clients. Personal histories and experiences are not necessary for the professional project, and may therefore be dispensed with on entering the field. Hence, the feeling among many participants that their racial identities – which point to experience and history different from that of colleagues whose bodies suggest homology – needs to be managed.

As Chapters 5 and 6 suggest, BAME practitioners are likely to adopt strategies reflecting the sense that race is better masked than overt in many interactions ('passing' by making race relatively less visible), is commodified in others (exploiting stereotypes by making visible race useful), and the threat it poses defused in still other circumstances. All three strategies allow their racialization to be managed in the occupational context, even though they may also involve an unpleasant construction of absence, an amputation of core identity. Moreover, managing racialization is essential not only to deflect unwanted attention from visible difference, but to redirect attention towards skills and attributes that meet or exceed occupational norms: commitment, hard work, track record, high-quality skills and talent, for example. These need to be more visible than race if BAME practitioners are to be successful, since they allow race to be overlooked, looked past, or simply matter less.

Visible skills need to be unproblematic, suggesting fit rather than difference. Skills that derived from difference are more difficult to claim as valuable: as Chapter 3 suggests, once societal interests are written out of the professional project, the space for BAME practitioners to bring their own social and cultural histories to bear on campaigns is also more limited. While some practitioners spoke positively about their roles as a means of helping organizations to reach different communities effectively (Chapter 6), such work was relatively uncommon. For the most part, the voices and experiences of audiences that do not immediately fit organizational objectives – frequently, those disadvantaged by their class and race – are obscured by the more immediate prospect of potential revenue, support or engagement from influential groups and individuals – frequently, those privileged by their class and race. The ability to engage with different reference points and life experiences often remained invisible, other than the infrequent occasions when organizational interests converged with this particular communicative skill.

For BAME practitioners, then, visibility is a complex juggling act, a balance between managing the 'grit' generated by their racialized identity in a way that makes their presence palatable for the field, and simultaneously bringing forth skills that demonstrate their fit with the occupational habitus and professionalization project, as forms of grease to ease their professional trajectory. Too much grease, however, and their racial identity resurfaced as a source of fear and instability when discovered in unexpected locations (as senior managers, directors, team leaders and budget holders). The opposite is true for white practitioners. As Chapter 5 shows, the heretical field constructed by participants in the study demonstrates how practitioners who can claim whiteness enjoy visibility that they do not have to work for or manage in the same way as BAME practitioners. Their skills are enhanced, rather than obscured, by the universality of their unmarked racial identity, their natural fit with the occupational habitus and their obvious contribution to PR's professionalization project. Once the arbitrary attribution of value to different bodies is made visible however, its power is lessened; it can become a starting point for active resistance, allowing BAME practitioners to challenge and manage their visibility in relation to the privilege that their colleagues attract.

Race-as-process/race-as-category

The construction of anything depends on stable foundations, so if race is to be a difference that matters, then it has to be built in categorical terms, less variable and fluid than race-as-process. Instances of race-as-category are not so easily identified in a post-race world, where racism is supposed to be a thing of the past (Bonilla-Silva, 2010). PR's occupational narrative, for example, ignores race and racism (along with other ethical and moral dimensions of the social world) as factors relevant to communication. Yet, the contrast is stark between the absence of race in occupational discourse and the prevalence of race-as-category in experiences of racialization in the field.

The analysis in this book focused on diversity as a socially constructed experience rather than simply a set of numbers or statistics. This directs attention to race-as-process, but also reveals the latter's unevenness and variability over time and in different spaces. As noted in Chapter 1, understanding race-as-process locates race in discursive and material contexts, a process of emergent meaning that varies as circumstances change. However, for the participants in the study, understanding their position in the field came from its repeated enforcement through individual incidents of implicit or explicit racism, based on categorical assumptions about identity. The common elements that connected participants' experiences of being racialized were grounded in static preconceptions about their subjectivity: the attribution of predictable stereotypes, for example, resulted in assumptions made about BAME practitioners' intellect, capability and suitability for different roles that they recognized and tackled on a regular basis. Similarly, white colleagues' assumptions of absolute, rather than relative difference created uncertainty around interactions that BAME practitioners tried to ameliorate. Thus, in PR, race-as-process (the construction and experience of race and racialization) is constituted through the repeated application of race-as-category (e.g. stereotyping or pigeonholing) at the intersubjective, organizational and institutional level.

Ironically, the predictability of discrimination derived from the treatment of race-as-category, while a potentially exhausting and sometimes disheartening experience, provided BAME practitioners with a relatively stable set of options to resist racialization. Their liminal understanding of whiteness meant they could read into the formulaic thinking that lay behind their treatment, and address it in subtle ways. Rarely did participants talk about direct conversations they had had about prejudice; more often, their narratives focused on the ways they manipulated implicit perceptions of their identity using the tools that the occupational field made available to them: certain valued forms of capital, skills, or networks, for example. While such strategies do invite complicity in PR's professionalization project, they are nonetheless a form of resistance. The centrality of whiteness as the foundation of PR's professionalization project, is both a source of hegemony and an achilles heel, in that its disciplinary prescriptions of identity may be consciously used to resist the racialization of the 'other'.

General/particular

The need to construct occupational archetypes of PR practice and practitioners as part of the field's professionalization project inevitably results in generalizations about the occupation and those who work in it, whether they are insiders or outsiders-within. As illustrated in Chapters 3 and 4, these generalizations relate to PR's expertise in a challenging communicative environment, its ability to serve a wide range of organizational interests through reputation management, and its promise of a close, dedicated client relationship through which those interests are understood and realized. Also generalized is the absence of a societally grounded morality and ethics as a foundation – or even a concern – for PR. Such generalizations facilitate PR's jurisdiction and legitimacy, and as long as they are evidenced by practitioners in some form, they make a significant contribution to the professionalization project.

As I have argued, it is more difficult for BAME practitioners to embody the archetypal practitioner, or to be seen as the source of archetypal practice because of the condensed subjectivities that accompany their bodies. Because PR's generalizations are marked by whiteness, they incorporate the deployment of race-as-category rather than race-as-process, divorced from day-to-day experience and abstracted from both context and subjectivity. Given that BAME practitioners are generally excluded from PR's archetypes (in contrast to the general inclusion of white bodies), the particularity of their work in specific campaigns has to be taken into account to make sense of their presence as a useful resource for PR's professionalization project: they must provide (more) evidence of their skills and contribution. Thus, generalized assumptions about PR's practice and practitioners, which discipline the field, inevitably invite illustrations of the particular from those whose presence contests their validity. Likewise, the importance of the particular is thrown into relief by the prevalence of generalized assumptions.

Like the other dialectics, the opposing poles are intimately connected in practice. Introducing the particular as a justification for inclusion requires time and effort on the part of both BAME practitioners, and those they interact with. However, it is an empowering process, not only because it allows BAME practitioners to demonstrate valued professional capabilities and skills, but also because it undermines the whiteness of PR's archetypes as grounds for both inclusion in the field, and for its legitimacy and jurisdiction. It points to the fact that the classed, racialized and gendered forms of whiteness that mark PR are neither inevitable nor necessary for PR to maintain its territory. As such, each time the strategy is successful, it furnishes BAME practitioners with new resources to protect themselves from, and challenge, racialization.

Options for change?

Examining diversity from a dialectical perspective underlines the fact that diversity is a struggle over identity and power and specifically, over claiming identities that deserve recognition and value from the occupational field. Miller and Rose (1995:

428) argue that 'transformations in identity [...] must address the practices that act on human beings and human conduct in specific domains of existence, and the systems of thought that underpin these practices and are embodied within them'. The dialectical approach adds to this by showing that different interpretations of PR practice and discourse contribute to our overall understanding of the issue of diversity. Reflecting on how 'others' are discursively constructed by the field reveals one side of the aforementioned four dialectics, but its effects cannot be understood without reference to the ways in which the status of 'other' can transform into that of an outsider-within who can use, incorporate and resist dominant narratives in his or her daily life. In the process of negotiating their way through a PR career, outsiders-within draw on resources that allow them to both challenge normative prescriptions of 'fit' in the field, and use those prescriptions to demonstrate their suitability for the occupation.

Being included in PR takes many forms: being visible, being valued, being equitably rewarded, being seen. On its most fundamental level, however, being included means having the right to articulate one's own understanding of the PR field, and have that narration heard and validated by one's colleagues. In other words, pursuing diversity in PR means accepting the human need in all practitioners to be recognized (Honneth, 1996) and valued in their sphere of work, and for their voices to matter, politically, in the field (Ahmed, 2012; Couldry, 2010). This means understanding the workplace not only as a place where we are economically productive, but also a place that links 'the sphere of production with the nature of democracy' (Miller and Rose, 1995: 428). It means changing our understanding of the PR field from an essentially economic engagement between individuals and organizations (a job, a means of building instrumental relationships, a process of constructing reputation), to a social and political engagement. The fact that fields are fundamentally relational is easily forgotten in the market-based thinking that tends to frame our understanding of what PR is about and why people choose to pursue it as a career, but understanding diversity as fundamentally democratic depends on us accepting a relational ontology for the field.

Interpreting diversity in PR as facilitating voice and recognition transforms diversity initiatives into (potentially) deeply democratic acts, driven by principles that extend beyond the business case in its particular PR guise. Their roots lie in the realization that the neoliberal economic and political principles to which PR is oriented, are an imperfect guide for constructing the field, since they fail to account for the reality that our social existence is inseparable from economics and politics, and therefore ignore the moral dimensions of our working lives (Couldry, 2010). In the current context, where discourses of terror and migration combine to both alienate 'new' strangers and conjure up once again the 'enemy within' of previous decades (Philo *et al.*, 2013; Ahmed, 2000), this lack of social awareness is particularly concerning. PR, as a communicative discipline, has the potential to be engaged with democracy as a 'genuinely heterogeneous space' (Hall, 2000: 235), connecting people, building relationships across communities, and creating stronger foundations for a society that caters to, rather than closes down, voice. We need to make more of this potential.

To be successful, then, diversity initiatives have to engage with the social and political dimensions of racialization in PR, rather than only the economic. Just as engaging with racism on a national level requires strategies that 'attempt to reconfigure or reimagine the nation *as a whole'* (Hall, 2000: 232, emphasis added) an agenda for change in PR needs to be 'transformative' at the institutional level in the sense suggested by Richards (2001: 18), addressing the need not only for marginalized groups to access power, but 'seek[ing] change in the nature of power itself'. The approach to understanding diversity taken in this book, that locates representations of whiteness and its 'others' in history and identifies the continuities of racialization across time and space, is a helpful starting point because it locates diversity, and makes visible its specific manifestations in peoples' lives, rather than treating it as an abstract concept. But how useful are such insights for really developing diversity in practice? Can they fundamentally change the 'infrasystem', in the way that Creedon (1991) argues is necessary for developing a more equitable field?

In response to such questions, it would be unrealistic and somewhat arrogant to propose a set of concrete strategies that will work miracles where other initiatives have failed. However, it is worth considering some principles that relate to the argument developed through this book, and may provide a stronger foundation for diversity work in PR in the future.

1   *Do not rely on the occupation to generate change*

The natural tendency of occupational fields to preserve the status quo, or pursue change only insofar as it facilitates power for those who already enjoy status and legitimacy, means that the impetus for change from the occupation itself will always be relatively weak. Greater diversity will only emerge from occupational initiatives if the field is compelled to engage seriously with the issue in order to retain its status *vis-à-vis* the individuals and institutions that lend it legitimacy and confirm its jurisdiction (e.g. clients, the media, corporate and political elites). While the business case explains the imperative for diversity in PR as part of the occupation's need to remain fluid and agile in response to a changing society, history shows that relying on the business case does not generate radical change. We may wait a long time for diversity to be so pressing an issue that it takes precedence over other occupational interests.

2   *Connect and make visible marginalized voices, to create a strong locus of change*

On the contrary, it is in the presence and work of 'outsiders-within' in and on the occupational field that the potential for change exists. The heretical interpretations BAME practitioners make of PR's dominant narratives, their understanding of how they are perceived and understood as PR practitioners, and the ways they manage their identities, are currently individual political acts. Yet, they offer great insight into the ways power works in the field, and they are connected by the historical patterns of racialization that mark some bodies as worth less than others. Institutional-level change may be a more realistic prospect if these acts of resistance can be connected and their deep critique of the field made more visible.

3   *Recognize race and racialization as process, rather than category*

For the critique of marginal voices in the field to be taken seriously, their experiences of discrimination must be recognized as part of a longer term process of racial identity construction, marked by historical norms and manifest through acts that differ in their intensity. The approach helps address the fact that discrimination is frequently difficult to pin down, but takes the form of accumulated and implicit marginalization across different places and at different times. For example, the importance of the microaggressions (Davis, 1989) that participants described – small but noticeable slights that are hard to both recognize and categorize as discrimination using a normative perspective of race-as-category – increases when each instance is understood in connection with others, rather than in isolation. Such steps also counter the occupational drive to minimize risks to its jurisdiction and legitimacy by distancing itself from the complexity of real life. They allow discrimination to move from an abstract possibility hinted at by statistics, to a specific set of located interactions that constitute evidence rather than simply events (Puwar, 2004).

4   *Treat diversity as an exercise in democracy*

Under what conditions would critique from the margins become a prompt for change, rather than exclusion? Only conditions that frame diversity in moral, rather than economic terms, since economic rationales for diversity, that situate the choice of whether or not to pursue diversity in the hands of employers and institutions, have limited longevity (Noon, 2007). Successful diversity management must begin by *sharing* discursive and material power, not giving opportunities for 'others' to have better lives *for themselves*. Diversity initiatives should be conceived as democratic initiatives, where everyone's voice is respected and heard. The occupational elite in PR must give credence to the voices of those who are marginalized in the field by allowing their narratives to stand alongside dominant archetypes – and displace hegemonic ideas where necessary.

5   *Take diversity as an opportunity for reflexivity*

The corollary of the previous point is that diversity requires PR's archetypes themselves to be opened up for scrutiny, since accepting heretical interpretations of the field is impossible without a willingness to destabilize whiteness among those who inhabit it. In other words, diversity must be understood to be about 'us' as much as it is about the 'other', and must make PR's particular form of whiteness strange (Dyer, 1997). If something is to be 'done' about diversity, then that something must also be understood as done to 'us', not just to 'them'. It is not possible to *find* space for diverse colleagues – space must be *made* for them; insiders have to make a conscious decision to take action that will facilitate change. As I have tried to illustrate in this book, space for the 'other' can only be constructed by first *deconstructing* normative representations of PR and its practitioners and revealing their flaws. Insiders in PR need to develop their own liminal knowledge about the whiteness of the field, the ways it constructs and disciplines them as practitioners, and the ways in which they are perceived by 'others' as a consequence. Genuine reflexivity will develop understanding of the ways in which insider status is dependent on marginalizing outsiders-within, and help practitioners cross the boundary that whiteness constructs between 'self' and 'other'.

In articulating these principles, I have in mind the effect this research might have on the practicalities of improving diversity in PR. However, the ways the principles are enacted in practice will depend on the specificities of the PR field in different geographies and in the context of different histories. It will also depend on the forms of racialization that mark the political, economic and social environment in which PR operates. In other words, researching and managing diversity must be located in the struggles over power and identity that shape the occupation at particular times and in particular places.

It follows that research on diversity in PR is most productively approached through a detailed investigation of the context for PR work. In this book, I took the occupational field as an important aspect of context that exercises significant power over the way that PR's identities and practices are constructed and, correspondingly, over the forms of exclusion that the field promotes. The approach has significant advantages in that it makes visible the logic behind occupational norms and explains the tendency towards inertia rather than change as a means of maintaining the occupation's status. The research has also focused in particular on discourse as a powerful representation of PR and its practitioners, and a disciplinary mechanism within the field. PR's habitus emerges as both a product of occupational discourses, enacting legitimate and valued representations of PR and its practitioners, and also a source of occupational discourse, since it validates such representations even as it reflects them.

To rely solely on occupational discourses as a means of understanding diversity in PR, however, would be to accept the categorical approach to race and identity that underpins them, and to ignore the importance of the dialectic between dominance and resistance that marks all power struggles (Foucault, 1980). Participants' narratives of PR revealed a different way of both conceptualizing race and racialization, defining their identities, and understanding and reading the field. Their alternative approach drew on their intersectional identities and liminal knowledge as sources of empowerment, and made space for them within the field as legitimate PR professionals. As I have already suggested such perspectives are crucial to any investigation of diversity since they provide essential resources for change.

In prioritising the occupational field, however, I have bypassed PR workplaces as sites where exclusion and inclusion are structured in particular ways, and indeed, where diversity initiatives have their concrete effects. To some extent, participants' narratives have illustrated the ways exclusion is enacted at an organizational level, but the picture remains one-sided. I have also spoken of 'the occupational field' as a singular entity, inevitably minimizing the variability within the field, and the good work on diversity that may well exist in some PR specialisms. Finally, I have spoken of BAME practitioners as a group whose members face the same or similar forms of discrimination. As noted in Chapter 2, my point is not that all BAME practitioners suffer the same kinds of discrimination (indeed, an intersectional approach to identity dictates against this), nor that all white practitioners enjoy privilege. The fact that whiteness is classed and gendered as much as it is raced means that practitioners can access some forms of whiteness even if they are not white (and participants discussed strategies that illustrated exactly this approach to managing their workplace identity). Equally, some white practitioners may be disadvantaged by virtue of a lack of certain desirable forms of capital. My point is that the subjectivities carried by BAME bodies as a result of the racialization such bodies have been subjected to over time, make them vulnerable to marginalization, even if it is not a constant feature of their working lives. Correspondingly, white bodies are more readily included in the field, even if they are also marginalized on occasion. We must, of course, recognize the fluidity of power and identity as mechanisms that shape the structures and experiences of PR in different ways for different people. But in doing so, we must not lose sight of the moral imperative to address the systemic racialization that marks PR – and that PR itself perpetuates – and take action to counter, and ultimately eliminate, its effects.

Notes

1 Introduction

1 While the term 'client' is traditionally used to refer to companies that employ consultants to do their PR work, for the purposes of simplification I use the term in this book to refer to both the companies (and their staff) that employ consultants, as well as to internal managers to whom PR staff report.

2 I place 'race' within quotes to indicate that it is a social construction rather than an absolute reality. Whenever the term race is used in this book, it is in the social constructionist sense. However, for reasons of style I do not repeat the inverted commas throughout the book.

3 Indeed, Witz (1992) argues that the term 'profession' is itself gendered, because it has historically referred to male-dominated, class-privileged occupations.

4 A cynic might point out that this focus was initiated only after damning and high-profile media coverage about PR interns working for up to six months without pay (Mattinson and Wicks, 2011), and following recent publicity about the fact that 'employing' an intern for more than a short period of time without pay is illegal (Mendelsohn, 2013).

5 The CIPR has initiated discussions about diversity in the occupation since the early 2000s, but these have had very little material impact on the numbers and positions of BAME practitioners.

6 Malik (2013) illustrates this point in the shift towards 'creative diversity' in public service broadcasting in the United Kingdom, a move that has removed the more political 'cultural diversity' from discussion and opened the door to the reification of creativity as a locus of economic return. It is a 'pro-creative, not pro-cultural vision' and links to the emphasis on creative industries as an important platform for Britain's global competitiveness. See Chapter 4 for a discussion of the importance of creativity in PR's occupational archetypes.

7 Couldry (2010) identifies two dimensions of voice: as process, or the act of giving an account of oneself, and voice as value, which points analyses to the contexts and conditions in which voice as process (i.e. the act of giving account and the account itself) matters and in which it is devalued. As he notes: 'Treating voice as a value means discriminating in favour of ways of organizing human life and resources that, through their choices, put the value of voice into practice, by respecting the multiple interlinked processes of voice and sustaining then, not undermining or denying them. Treating voice as value means discriminating against frameworks of social, economic and political organization that deny or undermine voice' (2010: 2). In this book, the occupational field may be understood as a framework within which voice may or may not be valued. The litmus test for diversity management initiatives, too, can be conceived as whether they facilitate voice as value, or merely as process.

2 Historical context: empire, racism and public relations

1 Other perspectives on social history will inform the experiences of (for example) women and men, gay and straight, religious and secular practitioners. In focusing on race as the primary category of difference in this study, I do not mean to imply that other histories, which intersect with the ones I investigate, are of no consequence. They are, but they are not the main focus of this work.

2 Ramamurthy (2003) and others have noted the importance of recognizing that essentialist representations of the 'other' by the British Empire were always contested by colonized populations, but Ramamurthy (2003: 7–8) points out that, in the context of advertising, control over the initial representational form lay with the advertisers and therefore was not open to resistance. The same applies to PR: while its meaning is always fluid once released into the social world, my interest here is in addressing the representations of Britain and the 'other' encoded into the text at the point of creation, as a means of understanding how PR was used to further the political and economic project of Empire.

3 It is worth noting that the CIPR awards the Stephen Tallents medal each year to recognize exceptional achievement in, and contributions to, the development of public relations practice by a CIPR member. One assumes the broader context of Tallents' work has only briefly been considered as a factor in naming the award after him, if at all. It's also worth pointing out that although only 37 per cent of the field are male, men make up 86 per cent, or 25 of the 29 medal recipients listed on the CIPR website (see http://www.cipr. co.uk/content/about-us/people/medal-winners).

4 While third sector organizations do use PR extensively, corporates and government enjoy important structural advantages in the public sphere, including extensive resources to invest in PR and symbolic authority in an environment where the status quo affirms their interests (Moloney, 2006). The influence of whiteness as a benchmark for PR work therefore tends to prevail.

3 Constructing PR practice: legitimacy, jurisdiction and the erasure of social inequity

1 While not all PR campaigns are specifically oriented towards consumption per se, audiences are increasingly treated as 'consumers' through the act of choosing to engage with a particular organization and use its 'product' from among a number of competitive options. Thus, even among political parties, NGOs and non-market institutions such as local councils, universities, and hospitals, audiences choose to 'consume' the product on offer, whether it is a policy, a degree programme, or an operation.

2 ESRC grant reference RES 000-22-3143.

5 Strategies of resistance: intersectional identities as a source of critique

1 Sue *et al.* (2007: 271) describe racial microaggressions as: 'brief and commonplace daily verbal, behavioral, or environmental indignities, whether intentional or unintentional, that communicate hostile, derogatory, or negative racial slights and insults toward people of color. Perpetrators of microaggressions are often unaware that they engage in such communications when they interact with racial/ethnic minorities'.

References

Abbott, A. 1988. *The System of Professions: An Essay on the Division of Expert Labour.* Chicago: University of Chicago Press.

Acker, J. 2006. Inequality regimes: Gender, class and race in organizations. *Gender & Society,* 20, 441–464.

Adib, A. and Guerrier, Y. 2003. The interlocking of gender with nationality, race, ethnicity and class: The narratives of women in Hotel Work. *Gender, Work and Organization,* 10, 413–433.

Ahmed, S. 2000. *Strange Encounters: Embodied Others in Postcoloniality.* London: Routledge.

Ahmed, S. 2006. *Queer Phenomenology: Orientations, Objects, Others.* Durham, NC: Duke University Press.

Ahmed, S. 2007a. The language of diversity. *Ethnic and Racial Studies,* 30, 235–256.

Ahmed, S. 2007b. 'You end up doing the document rather than doing the doing': Diversity, race equality and the politics of documentation. *Ethnic and Racial Studies,* 30, 590–609.

Ahmed, S. 2009. Embodying diversity: Problems and paradoxes for Black feminists. *Race, Ethnicity and Education,* 12, 41–52.

Ahmed, S. 2012. *On Being Included: Racism and Diversity in Institutional Life.* Durham, NC: Duke University Press.

Aitken, I. 1990. *Film and Reform: John Grierson and the Documentary Film Movement.* London: Routledge.

Aldoory, L. 2003. The empowerment of feminist scholarship in public relations and the building of a feminist paradigm. *Communication Yearbook,* 27, 221–255.

Aldoory, L. 2007. Reconceiving gender for an 'Excellent' future in public relations scholarship. *In:* Toth, E. (ed.) *The Future of Excellence in Public Relations and Communication Mangement: Challenges for the Next Generation.* Mahwah, NJ: Lawrence Erlbaum.

Aldoory, L. and Toth, E. 2002. Gender discrepancies in a gendered profession: A developing theory for public relations. *Journal of Public Relations Research,* 14, 103–126.

Aldridge, M. and Evetts, J. 2003. Rethinking the concept of professionalism: The case of journalism. *British Journal of Sociology,* 54, 547–564.

Alexander, B. K. 2004. Black skin/White masks: The performative sustainability of Whiteness (with apologies to Franz Fanon). *Qualitative Inquiry,* 10, 647–672.

Alexander, C. 2006. Introduction: Mapping the issues. *Ethnic and Racial Studies,* 29, 397–410.

Alvesson, M. 1994. Talking in organizations: Managing identity and impressions in an advertising agency. *Organization Studies,* 15, 535–563.

Alvesson, M. and Johansson, A. W. 2002. Professionalism and politics in management consultancy work. *In:* Clark, T. and Fincham, R. (eds.) *Critical Consulting: New Perspectives on the Management Advice Industry.* Oxford: Blackwell.

Anderson-Gough, F., Grey, C. and Robson, K. 1998. Work hard, play hard: An analysis of organizational cliche in two accountancy practices. *Organization*, 5, 565–592.

Anderson-Gough, F., Grey, C. and Robson, K. 2000. In the name of the client: The service ethic in two professional services firms. *Human Relations,* 53, 1151–1174.

Anderson-Gough, F., Grey, C. and Robson, K. 2005. 'Helping them to forget..': The organizational embedding of gender relations in public audit firms. *Accounting, Organizations and Society,* 30, 469–490.

Anderson-Gough, F., Grey, C. and Robson, K. 2006. Professionals, networking and the networked professional. *Research in the Sociology of Organizations*, 24, 231–256.

Anthias, F. 2001. The concept of 'social division' and theorising social stratification: Looking at ethnicity and class. *Sociology,* 35, 835–854.

Anthias, F. 2013. Intersectional what? Social divisions, intersectionality and levels of analysis. *Ethnicities,* 13, 3–19.

Anthony, S. 2012. *Public Relations and the Making of Modern Britain: Stephen Tallents and the Birth of a Progressive Media Profession.* Manchester: Manchester University Press.

Appadurai, A. 1996. *Modernity at Large: Cultural Dimensions of Globalization.* Minneapolis: University of Minnesota Press.

Arts Council England. 2008. *Diversity in Publishing Programme Evaluation.* London: Arts Council England.

Ashcraft, K. 2007. Appreciating the 'work' of discourse: Occupational identity and difference as organizing mechanisms in the case of commercial airline pilots. *Discourse & Communication,* 1, 9–36.

Atewologun, D. and Singh, V. 2010. Challenging ethnic and gender identities: An exploration of UK black professionals' identity construction. *Equality, Diversity and Inclusion: An International Journal,* 29, 332–347.

Bagilhole, B. and Goode, J. 2001. The contradiction of the myth of individual merit and the reality of a patriarchal support system in academic careers: A feminist investigation. *European Journal of Women's Studies,* 8, 161–180.

Bailey, R. and Thompson, R. 2012. A case study of public relations practice in 10 Downing Street during the Thatcher Government from 1980–1981. *In:* Watson, T. (ed.) *The International History of Public Relations Conference.* Bournemouth: Bournemouth University.

Balaji, M. 2009. Why do good girls have to be bad? The cultural industry's production of the Other and the complexities of agency. *Popular Communication: The International Journal of Media and Culture,* 7, 225–236.

Banks, S. P. 2000. *Multicultural Public Relations: A Social-Interpretive Approach.* Iowa: Iowa State University Press.

Bauman, Z. 1998. *Globalization: The Human Consequences.* Cambridge: Polity Press.

Becker, H. S. 1970. *Sociological Work: Method and Substance.* Chicago: Aldine Publishing.

Becker, H. S., Geer, E., Hughes, E. and Strauss, A. L. 2009 [1961]. *Boys in White: Student Culture in Medical School.* Chicago: University of Chicago Press.

Bell, D. 1980. *Brown v Board of Education* and the interest covergence dilemma. *Harvard Law Review,* 93, 518–533.

bell hooks. 1994. *Outlaw Culture: Resisting Representations.* London: Routledge.

Bell Pottinger. 2010. *Collaboration* [Online]. London: Bell Pottinger. Available at: http://www.bell-pottinger.co.uk/how_we_work.html [accessed 4 January 2010].

Bilge, S. 2010. Recent feminist outlooks on intersectionality. *Diogenes,* 225, 58–72.

Boltanski, L. and Thevenot, L. 2006[1991]. *On Justification: Economies of Worth.* Princeton: Princeton University Press.

Bolton, S. and Muzio, D. 2007. Can't live with 'em; Can't live without 'em: Gendered segmentation in the legal profession. *Sociology,* 41, 47–64.

Bolton, S. and Muzio, D. 2008. The paradoxical processes of feminization in the professions: The case of established, aspiring and semi-professions. *Work, Employment and Society,* 22, 281–299.

Bonilla-Silva, E. 2010. *Racism Without Racists: Color-Blind Racism and Racial Inequality in Contemporary America.* Lanham, MD: Rowman and Littlefield.

Boogard, B. and Roggeband, C. 2010. Paradoxes of intersectionality: Theorizing inequality in the Dutch police force through structure and agency. *Organization,* 17, 53–75.

Bourdieu, P. 1984. *Distinction: A Social Critique of the Judgement of Taste.* London: Routledge & Kegan Paul.

Bourdieu, P. 1991. *Language and Symbolic Power.* Cambridge, UK: Polity Press.

Bourdieu, P. 1992. *The Field of Cultural Production: Essays in Art and Literature.* Cambridge: Polity Press.

Bourdieu, P. 1997. The forms of capital. *In:* Halsey, A. H., Lauder, H., Brown, P. and Stuart Wells, A. (eds.) *Education, Culture, Economy, Society.* Oxford: Oxford University Press.

Bourdieu, P. 2000. *Pascalian Meditations.* Stanford, CA: Stanford University Press/Polity Press.

Bourne, C. 2003. The UK's minority-owned PR firms – players without networks? *In: Current Debates and Issues in Public Relations Research and Practice.* Poole: Bournemouth University.

Brah, A. 1992. Difference, diversity and differentiation. *In:* Donald, J. and Rattansi, A. (eds.) *Race, Culture and Difference.* London: Sage.

Brah, A. and Phoenix, A. 2004. 'Ain't I A Woman': Revisiting intersectionality. *Journal of International Women's Studies,* 5, 75–86.

Brewis, J. and Grey, C. 1994. Re-eroticizing the organization: An exegesis and critique. *Gender, Work and Organization,* 1, 67–82.

Bridgen, L. 2011. Emotional labour and the pursuit of the personal brand: Public relations practitioners' use of social media. *Journal of Media Practice,* 12, 61–76.

British Medical Association. 2009. *Equality and diversity in UK medical schools.* London: British Medical Association.

Carastathis, A. 2008. The invisibility of privilege: A critique of intersectional models of identity. *Les Ateliers de l'Ethique,* 3, 23–38.

Carbado, D. and Gulati, M. 2003. The law and economics of critical race theory. *The Yale Law Journal,* 112, 1757–1828.

Carbado, D. and Gulati, M. 2013. *Acting White: Rethinking Race in Post-Racial America.* New York: Oxford University Press.

Castells, M. 2000. *The Rise of the Networked Society.* Oxford: Blackwell.

Centre for Economics and Business Research Ltd. 2005. *PR Today: 48,000 professionals; £6.5 billion turnover.* London: Centre for Economics and Business Research Ltd.

Chang, R. 2002. Critiquing 'race' and its uses: Critical race theory's uncompleted argument. *In:* Valdes, F., Mccristal Culp, J. and Harris, A. P. (eds.) *Crossroads, Directions and a New Critical Race Theory.* Philadelphia: Temple University Press.

Chartered Institute of Public Relations. 2006. *The Business of Diversity.* London: Chartered Institute of Public Relations.

Chartered Institute of Public Relations. 2009a. *About PR* [Online]. London: Chartered Institute of Public Relations. Available at: http://www.cipr.co.uk/content/about-us/about-pr [accessed 4 October 2011].

Chartered Institute of Public Relations. 2009b. *CIPR Diversity Policy* [Online]. London: Chartered Institute of Public Relations. Available at: http://www.cipr.co.uk/diversity/policy/policymain.asp [accessed 3 April 2009].

Chartered Institute of Public Relations. 2011a. *Is PR for you?* [Online]. London: Chartered Institute of Public Relations. Available at: http://www.cipr.co.uk/content/careers/careers-advice [accessed 19 December 2011].

Chartered Institute of Public Relations. 2011b. *Value of PR* [Online]. London: Chartered Institute of Public Relations [accessed 19 December 2011].

Chartered Institute of Public Relations. 2012. *Diversity Strategy* [Online]. London: Chartered Institute of Public Relations. Available at: http://www.cipr.co.uk/content/policy-resources/diversity-strategy [accessed 14 December 2012].

Chartered Institute of Public Relations. 2013a. *About PR* [Online]. London: Chartered Institute of Public Relations. Available at: http://www.cipr.co.uk/content/about-us/about-pr [accessed 31 October 2013].

Chartered Institute of Public Relations. 2013b. *Code of Conduct.* London: Chartered Institute of Public Relations.

Chartered Institute of Public Relations. 2013c. *Public Relations Professionals to Discuss the Business Case for Diversity* [Online]. London: Chartered Institute of Public Relations. Available at: http://newsroom.cipr.co.uk/public-relations-professionals-to-discuss-the-business-case-for-diversity/ [accessed 4 January 2014].

CitigateDeweRogerson. 2010. *Investor Relations* [Online]. London: CitigateDeweRogerson. Available at: http://www.citigatedewerogerson.com/investor_relations.html [accessed 4 January 2010].

Claringbould, I., Knoppers, A. and Elling, A. 2004. Exclusionary practices in sport journalism. *Sex Roles,* 51, 709–718.

Coates, R. 2006. Introduction. *In:* Coates, R. (ed.) *Race and Ethnicity: Across Time, Space and Discipline.* Leiden: Koninklijke Brill NV.

Coates, R. 2008. Covert racism in the USA and globally. *Sociology Compass,* 2, 208–231.

Cohen, L., Wilkinson, A., Arnold, J. and Finn, R. 2005. 'Remember I'm the bloody architect!': Architects, organizations and discourses of profession. *Work, Employment & Society,* 19, 775–796.

Cole, M. 2004. 'Brutal and stinking' and 'difficult to handle': The historical and contemporary manifestations of racialisation, institutional racism, and schooling in Britain. *Race, Ethnicity and Education,* 7, 35–56.

Cottle, S. 1998. Making ethnic minority programmes inside the BBC: Professional pragmatics and cultural containment. *Media,Culture and Society,* 20, 295–317.

Cottle, S. (ed.) 2000. *Ethnic Minorities and the Media: Changing Cultural Boundaries.* Buckingham: Open University Press.

Couldry, N. 2010. *Why Voice Matters: Culture and Politics After Neoliberalism.* London: Sage.

Creegan, C., Colgan, F., Charlesworth, R. and Robinson, G. 2003. Race equality policies at work: Employee perceptions of the 'implementation gap' in a UK local authority. *Work, Employment and Society,* 17, 617–640.

Crenshaw, K. 1989. Demarginalizing the intersection of race and sex: A Black feminist critique of antidiscrimination doctrine, feminist theory, and antiracist politics. *University of Chicago Legal Forum,* 1989, 139–167.

Crenshaw, K. W. 1991. Mapping the margins: Intersectionality, identity politics, and violence against women of color. *Stanford Law Review,* 43, 1241–1299.

David, P. 2004. Extending symmetry: Toward a convergence of professionalism, practice, and pragmatics in public relations. *Public Relations Research,* 16, 185–211.

Davidson, M. J. and Burke, R. J. 2004. Women in management worldwide: Facts, figures and analysis – An overview. *In:* Davidson, M. J. and Burke, R. J. (eds.) *Women in Management Worldwide: Facts, Figures and Analysis.* Aldershot, UK: Ashgate.

Davis, A. 2003. Whither mass media and power? Evidence for a critical elite theory alternative. *Media, Culture and Society,* 25, 669–690.

Davis, K. 2008. Intersectionality as buzzword: A sociology of science perspective on what makes a feminist theory successful. *Feminist Theory,* 9, 67–85.

Davis, P. 1989. Law as microaggression. *Yale Law Journal,* 98, 1559–1577.

Daymon, C. and Demetrious, K. 2010. Gender and public relations: Perspectives, applications and questions [Online]. *PRism,* 7. Available at: http://www.prismjournal.org/fileadmin/Praxis/Files/Gender/Daymon_Demetrious.pdf

Daymon, C. and Demetrious, K. (eds.) 2013. *Gender and Public Relations: Critical Perspectives on Voice, Image, and Identity.* London: Routledge.

Delgado, R. and Stefancic, J. 2001. *Critical Race Theory: An Introduction.* New York: New York University Press.

Dhamoon, R. 2011. Considerations on mainstreaming intersectionality. *Political Research Quarterly,* 64, 230–243.

Dozier, D. M. and Broom, G. M. 1995. Evolution of the manager role in public relations practice. *Journal of Public Relations Research,* 7, 3–26.

Du Gay, P. and Salaman, G. 1992. The cult[ure] of the customer. *Journal of Management Studies,* 29, 615–633.

Du Bois, W. E. B. 1903. *The Souls of Black Folk.* New York: Bantam Classic.

Dyer, R. 1997. *White.* New York: Routledge.

Edelman. 2010. *Corporate Reputation* [Online]. London: Edelman. Available at: http://www.edelman.co.uk/what-we-do/corporate-reputation [accessed 5 January 2010].

Edwards, L. 2008. PR practitioners' cultural capital: An initial study and implications for research and practice. *Public Relations Review,* 34, 367–372.

Edwards, L. 2013. Institutional racism in cultural production: The case of public relations. *Popular Communication: The International Journal of Media and Culture,* 11, 242–256.

Ely, R. and Thomas, D. A. 2001. Cultural diversity at work: The effects of diversity perspectives on work group processes and outcomes. *Administrative Science Quarterly,* 46, 229–273.

Equality Act. 2010. *Equality Act.* London: The Stationery Office.

Essed, P. 1991. *Understanding Everyday Racism.* London: Sage.

Evetts, J. 2011. A new professionalism? Challenges and opportunities. *Current Sociology,* 59, 406–422.

Ewen, S. 1996. *PR! A Social History of Spin.* New York: Basic Books.

Fairclough, N. 2003. *Analysing Discourse: Textual Analysis for Social Research.* London: Routledge.

Faist, T. 2009. Diversity: A new mode of incorporation? *Ethnic and Racial Studies,* 32, 171–190.

Fanon, F. 2008(1952). *Black Skin, White Masks.* London: Pluto Press.

Farmbrough, H. 2009. It does matter. *Accountancy Magazine,* 22–23.

Fishburn Hedges. 2010a. *About Us* [Online]. London: Fishburn Hedges. Available at: http://www.fishburn-hedges.com/aboutus [accessed 4 January 2010].

Fishburn Hedges. 2010b. *Message Development and Media Training* [Online]. London: Fishburn Hedges. Available at: http://www.fishburn-hedges.com/whatwedo/message developmentandmediatraining/ [accessed 5 January 2010].

Fishburn Hedges. 2010c. *What We Do: Emergency Relations* [Online]. London: Fishburn Hedges. Available at: http://www.fishburn-hedges.com/whatwedo/emergencyrelations/ [accessed 5 January 2010].

Fitch, K. and Third, A. 2010. Working girls: Revisiting the gendering of public relations [Online]. *PRism*, 7. Available at: http://www.prismjournal.org/fileadmin/Praxis/Files/Gender/Fitch_Third.pdf

Flintoff, A., Fitzgerald, H. and Scraton, S. 2008. The challenges of intersectionality: Researching difference in physical education. *International Studies in Sociology of Education*, 18, 73–85.

Flood, J. 2011. The re-landscaping of the legal profession: Large law firms and professional re-regulation. *Current Sociology*, 59, 507–529.

Ford, R. and Appelbaum, L. 2009. *Multicultural survey of PR practitioners* [Online]. New York: City College of New York. Available at: http://www.ccny.cuny.edu/prsurvey [accessed 22 September 2009].

Foucault, M. 1980. *Power/Knowledge*. Hemel Hempstead, UK: Harvester Press Ltd.

Foucault, M. 1991. Governmentality. *In:* Burchell, G., Gordon, C. and Miller, P. (eds.) *The Foucault Effect: Studies in Governmentality*. Chicago: Chicago University Press.

Fournier, V. 1999. The appeal to 'professionalism' as a disciplinary mechanism. *The Sociological Review*, 47, 280–307.

Fraga, L., Martinez-Ebers, V., Lopez, L. and Ramirez, R. 2006. *Strategic Intersectionality: Gender, Ethnicity, and Political Incorporation*. Berkeley, CA: Institute of Governmental Studies.

Frankenberg, R. 1993. *White Women, Race Matters: The Social Construction of Whiteness*. Minneapolis, MN: University of Minnesota Press.

Freud Communications. 2010a. *Freud Communications* [Online]. London: Freud Group. Available at: www.freud.com [accessed 4 January 2010].

Freud Communications. 2010b. *Our People* [Online]. London: Freud Communications. Available at: www.freud.com [accessed 4 January 2010].

Friedson, E. 2001. *Professionalism: The Third Logic*. Chicago, IL: University of Chicago Press.

Fuss, D. 1989. *Essentially Speaking: Feminism, Nature and Difference*. New York: Routledge.

Gallicano, T. 2013. Millenials' perceptions about diversity in their PR agencies. *Public Relations Journal*, 7, 37–70.

Giddens, A. 1999. *Runaway World: How Globalisation is Shaping Our Lives*. London: Profile.

Gillborn, D. 2008. *Racism and Education: Coincidence or Conspiracy?* Abingdon, UK: Routledge.

Gilroy, P. 1987. *There Ain't No Black in the Union Jack: The Cultural Politics of Race and Nation*. London: Routledge.

Gilroy, P. 1993. *The Black Atlantic: Modernity and Double-Consciousness*. Boston, MA: Harvard University Press.

Gilroy, P. 2004. *After Empire: Melancholia or Convivial Culture?* Abingdon, UK: Routledge.

Gilroy, P. 2010. *Darker Than Blue: On the Moral Economies of Black Atlantic Culture*. Boston, MA: Harvard University Press.

Gray, C. and Leith, H. 2004. Perpetuating gender stereotypes in the classroom: A teacher perspective. *Educational Studies*, 30, 3–17.

Grey, C. 1998. On being a professional in a 'Big Six' firm. *Accounting, Organizations and Society*, 23, 569–587.

Grimes, D. 2002. Challenging the status quo? Whiteness in the diversity management literature. *Management Communication Quarterly*, 15, 381–409.

Grunig, J. E. 1992. *Excellence in Public Relations and Communication Management*. Hillsdale, NJ: Lawrence Erlbaum.

Gunaratnam, Y. 2003. *Researching 'Race' and Ethnicity: Methods, Knowledge and Power*. London: Sage.

Gunnarsson, B.-L. 2009. *Professional Discourse*. London: Continuum.

Hall, S. 1988a. *The Hard Road to Renewal: Thatcherism and the Crisis of the Left*. London: Verso.

Hall, S. 1988b. New ethnicities. *In:* Mercer, K. (ed.) *Black Film/British Cinema*. London: Institute of Contemporary Arts.

Hall, S. 1993. What is this "Black" in Black popular culture? *Social Justice*, 20, 104–114.

Hall, S. 1996. Who needs 'identity'? *In:* Hall, S. and Du Gay, P. (eds.) *Questions Of Cultural Identity*. London: Sage.

Hall, S. 1997. *Representation: Cultural Representations and Signifying Practices*. London: Sage/Open University.

Hall, S. 2000. Conclusion: The multi-cultural question. *In:* Hesse, B. (ed.) *Un/settled Multiculturalisms*. London: Zed Books.

Hall, S., Critcher, C., Jefferson, T., Clarke, J. and Roberts, B. 2013. *Policing the Crisis: Mugging, the State and Law and Order* (2nd ed.). Basingstoke: Palgrave Macmillan.

Hammond, T., Clayton, B. and Arnold, P. 2012. South Africa's transition from apartheid: The role of professional closure in the experiences of black chartered accountants. *Accounting, Organizations and Society*, 34, 705–721.

Hancock, A. 2007. When multiplication doesn't equal quick addition: Examining intersectionality as a research paradigm. *Perspectives on Politics*, 5, 63–79.

Hanlon, G. 1999a. *Lawyers, the State and the Market: Professionalism Revisited*. London: Macmillan.

Hanlon, G. 1999b. Professionalism as enterprise – Service class politics and the redefinition of professionalism. *Sociology*, 32, 43–63.

Hanlon, G. 2004. Institutional forms and organizational structures: Homology, trust and reputational capital in professional service firms. *Organization*, 11, 187–210.

Harris, C. 1993. Whiteness as property. *Harvard Law Review*, 106, 1707–1791.

Harvey, D. 2005. *A Brief History of Neoliberalism*. Oxford: Oxford University Press.

Hesmondhalgh, D. and Baker, S. 2008. Creative work and emotional labour in the television industry. *Theory, Culture & Society*, 25, 97–118.

Hesse, B. 2000. Introduction: Un/settled multiculturalisms. *In:* Hesse, B. (ed.) *Un/settled Multiculturalisms: Diasporas, Entanglements, Transruptions*. London: Zed Books.

Hill-Collins, P. 1990. *Black Feminist Thought: Knowledge, Consciousness and the Politics of Empowerment*. London: Harper-Collins.

Hill and Knowlton. 2010. *Every Day Our Campaigns Change Behaviour* [Online]. London: Hill and Knowlton. Available at: http://www.hillandknowlton.co.uk/why/the-agency-behind-the-work [accessed 4 January 2010].

Hochschild, A. 1983. *The Managed Heart: The Commercialization of Human Feeling*. Berkeley, CA: University of California Press.

Hodgson, D. 2002. Disciplining the professional: The case of project management. *Journal of Management Studies,* 39, 803–821.

Hodgson, D. 2007. The new professionals: professionalisation and the struggle for occupational control in the field of project management. *In:* Muzio, D., Ackroyd, S. and Chanlat, J. (eds.) *Redirections in the Study of Expert Labour: Medicine, Law and Management Consultancy.* Basingstoke, UK: Palgrave.

Holtzhausen, D. 2012. *Public Relations as Activism: Postmodern Approaches to Theory and Practice.* London: Routledge.

Holvino, E. 2008. Intersections: The simultaneity of race, gender and class in Organization Studies. *Gender, Work and Organization,* 17, 248–277.

Hon, L. C. and Brunner, B. 2000. Diversity issues and public relations. *Journal of Public Relations Research,* 12, 309–340.

Honneth, A. 1996. *The Struggle for Recognition: The Moral Grammar of Social Conflicts.* Cambridge: Polity Press.

Hoque, K. and Noon, M. 2004. Equal opportunities policy and practice in Britain: Evaluating the 'empty shell' hypothesis. *Work, Employment and Society,* 18, 481–506.

Hulko, W. 2009. The time- and context-contingent nature of intersectionality and interlocking oppressions. *Affilia,* 24, 44–55.

Hurtado, A. 1996. Strategic suspensions: Feminists of color theorize the production of knowledge. *In:* Goldberger, N., Tarule, J., Clinchy, B. and Belenky, M. (eds.) *Knowledge, Difference and Power: Essays Inspired by Women's Ways of Knowing.* New York: Basic Books.

Hutnyk, J. 2006. Hybridity. *Ethnic and Racial Studies,* 28, 79–102.

Hutton, J. G. 2010. Defining the relationship between public relations and marketing: Public relations' most important challenge. *In:* Heath, R. (ed.) *The Sage Handbook of Public Relations.* Thousand Oaks, CA: Sage.

Hylton, K. 2009. *'Race' and Sport: Critical Race Theory.* London: Routledge.

Ihlen, O. 2005. The power of social capital: Adapting Bourdieu to the study of public relations. *Public Relations Review,* 31, 492–496.

Ihlen, O. 2007. Building on Bourdieu: A sociological grasp of public relations. *Public Relations Review,* 33, 269–274.

Johns, N. and Green, A. 2009. Equality, equal opportunities and diversity: Obfuscation as social justice. *Equal Opportunities International,* 28, 289–303.

Johnson, T. J. 1972. *Professions and Power.* London: Macmillan.

Jordan-Zachery, J. 2007. Am I a Black woman or a woman who is Black? A few thoughts on the meaning of intersectionality. *Politics and Gender,* 3, 254–263.

Kamenou, N. 2008. Reconsidering work-life balance debates: Challenging limited understandings of the 'life' component in the context of ethnic minority women's experiences. *British Journal of Management,* 19, 99–109.

Kay, F. and Hagan, J. 1998. Raising the bar: The gender stratification of law-firm capital. *American Sociological Review,* 63, 728–743.

Kern-Foxworth, M. 1989. Status and roles of minority PR practitioners. *Public Relations Review,* 15, 39–47.

Kern-Foxworth, M., Gandy, O., Hines, B. and Miller, D. A. 1994. Assessing the managerial roles of black female public relations practitioners using individual and organizational discriminants. *Journal of Black Studies,* 24, 416–434.

King, D. 1988. Multiple jeopardy, multiple consciousness: The context of a Black feminist ideology. *Signs,* 14, 42–72.

Kipping, M., Kirkpatrick, I. and Muzio, D. 2006. Overly controlled or out of control? Management consultants and the new corporate professionalism. *In:* Craig, J. (ed.) *Production Values: Futures for Professionalism.* London: Demos.

Kirton, G. 2009. Career plans and aspirations of recent black and minority ethnic business graduates. *Work, Employment & Society,* 23, 12–19.

Korczynski, M. 2003. Communities of coping: Collective emotional labour in service work. *Organization,* 10, 55–79.

Kyriacou, O. and Johnston, R. 2011. Exploring inclusion, exclusion and ethnicities in the institutional structures of U.K. accountancy. *Equality, Diversity and Inclusion: An International Journal,* 30, 482–497.

L'Etang, J. 2004. *Public Relations in Britain: A History of Professional Practice in the 20th Century.* Mahwah, NJ: Lawrence Erlbaum Associates.

L'Etang, J. 2006. Public relations as theatre: Key players in the evolution of British public relations. *In:* L'Etang, J. and Pieczka, M. (eds.) *Public Relations: Critical Debates and Contemporary Practice.* Mahwah, NJ: Lawrence Erlbaum Associates.

Ladson-Billings, G. 1999. Just what is critical race theory and what's it doing in a *nice* field like education? *In:* Parker, L., Deyhle, D. and Villenas, S. (eds.) *Race Is... Race Isn't: Critical Race Theory and Qualitative Studies in Education.* Boulder, CO: Westview Press.

Ladson-Billings, G. 2000. Racialized discourses and ethnic epistemologies. *In:* Denzin, N. K. and Lincoln, Y. S. (eds.) *The Handbook of Qualitative Research.* Thousand Oaks, CA: Sage.

Ladson-Billings, G. 2009. 'Who you callin' nappy-headed?' A critical race theory look at the construction of Black women. *Race, Ethnicity and Education,* 12, 87–99.

Ladson-Billings, G. and Donnor, J. 2008. The moral activist role of critical race theory scholarship. *In:* Denzin, N. K. and Lincoln, Y. S. (eds.) *The Sage Handbook of Qualitative Research.* Thousand Oaks, CA: Sage.

Lages, C. and Simkin, L. 2003. The dynamics of public relations: Key constructs and the drive for professionalism at the practitioner, consultancy and industry levels. *European Journal of Marketing,* 37, 298–328.

Larson, M. 1977. *The Rise of Professionalism: A Sociological Analysis.* Berkeley, CA: University of California Press.

Lash, S. and Urry, J. 1994. *Economies of Signs and Space.* London: Sage.

Lawrence, E. 1982. Just plain common sense: The roots of racism. *In:* Center for Contemporary Cultural Studies (ed.) *The Empire Strikes Back.* London: Hutchinson/ Routledge.

Leiss, W., Kline, S. and Jhally, S. 1997. *Social Communication in Advertising: Persons, Products and Images of Well-Being.* London: Routledge.

Len-Rios, M. 1998. Minority public relations practitioner perceptions. *Public Relations Review,* 24, 535–555.

Leveson, B. 2012. *An Inquiry into the Culture, Practices and Ethics of the Press: Report.* London: The Stationery Office.

Levine-Rasky, C. 2011. Intersectionality theory applied to whiteness and middle-classness. *Social Identities: Journal for the Study of Race, Nation and Culture,* 17, 239–253.

Lewis, J., Wren, M., Williams, A. and Franklin, R. 2008. A compromised Fourth Estate? UK news journalism, public relations and news sources. *Journalism Studies,* 9, 1–20.

Liff, S. 1997. Two routes to managing diversity: Individual differences or social group characteristics. *Employee Relations* 19, 11–26.

Logan, N. 2011. The White Leader prototype: A critical analysis of race in public relations. *Journal of Public Relations Research,* 23, 442–457.

Macpherson, W. 1999. *The Stephen Lawrence Inquiry.* London: The Stationery Office.

Malik, S. 2013. "Creative diversity": UK public service broadcasting after multiculturalism. *Popular Communication: The International Journal of Media and Culture,* 11, 227–241.

Martin, J. and Nakayama, T. 1999. Thinking dialectically about culture and commmunication. *Communication Theory,* 9, 1–25.

Mattinson, A. and Wicks, N. 2011. Leading fashion PR agency Modus Publicity targeted in BBC expose. *PR Week.* London: Haymarket. Available at: http://www.prweek.com/article/1052711/leading-fashion-pr-agency-modus-publicity-targeted-bbc-expose [accessed 5 January 2014].

Maynard, M. 1995. Race, gender and the concept of difference in feminist thought. *In:* Afshar, H. and Maynard, M. (eds.) *The Dynamics of Race and Gender: Some Feminist Interventions.* London: Taylor & Francis.

McCall, L. 2005. The complexity of intersectionality. *Signs: Journal of Women in Culture & Society,* 30, 1771–1800.

McClintock, A. 1995. *Imperial Leather: Race, Gender and Sexuality in the Colonial Conquest.* New York: Routledge.

McIntosh, P. 1997. White privilege and male privilege: A personal account of coming to correspondences through work in Women's Studies. *In:* Delgado, R. and Stefancic, J. (eds.) *Critical White Studies: Looking Behind the Mirror.* Philadelphia: Temple University Press.

McIntyre, A. 1997. *Making Meaning of Whiteness: Exploring Racial Identity with White Teachers.* New York, State University of New York Press.

McKinney, K. D. 2005. *Being White: Stories of Race and Racism.* New York: Routledge.

Mendelsohn, T. 2013. HMRC will investigate firms advertising for interns – to ensure they pay minimum wage. *The Independent.* Available at: http://www.independent.co.uk/student/news/hmrc-will-investigate-firms-advertising-for-interns--to-ensure-they-pay-minimum-wage-8932062.html [accessed 5 January 2014].

Miller, D. and Dinan, W. 2008. *A Century of Spin: How Public Relations Became the Cutting Edge of Corporate Power.* London: Pluto Press.

Miller, P. and Rose, N. 1990. Governing economic life. *Economy and Society,* 19, 1–31.

Miller, P. and Rose, N. 1995. Production, identity and democracy. *Theory and Society,* 24, 427–467.

Mirza, H. 2006. Transcendence over diversity: Black women in the academy. *Policy Futures in Education,* 4, 101–113.

Moloney, K. 2006. *Rethinking Public Relations: PR Propaganda and Democracy.* Oxon, UK: Routledge.

Mumby, D. K. and Stohl, C. 1991. Power and discourse in organization studies: Absence and the dialectic of control. *Discourse and Society,* 2, 313–332.

Munshi, D. and Edwards, L. 2011. Understanding 'race' in/and public relations: Where do we start from and where should we go? *Journal of Public Relations Research,* 23, 349–367.

Munshi, D. and Kurian, P. 2005. Imperializing spin cycles: A postcolonial look at public relations, greenwashing, and the separation of publics. *Public Relations Review,* 31, 513–520.

Munshi, D. and McKie, D. 2001. Different bodies of knowledge: Diversity and diversification in Public Relations. *Australian Journal of Communication,* 28, 11–22.

Muslim Council of Britain. 2013a. *Fear and Loathing Is Not the Best Response to Terrorism* [Online]. London: Muslim Council of Britain. Available at: http://www.mcb.

org.uk/index.php?option=com_content&view=article&id=2425:fear-and-loathing-is-not-the-best-response-to-terrorism-muslim-council-of-britain-responds-to-extremism-task-force-proposals&catid=40:press-release [accessed 22 December 2013].

Muslim Council of Britain. 2013b. *Muslim Council of Britain welcomes Baroness Warsi's robust defence of Islam and Muslims* [Online]. London: Muslim Council of Britain. Available at: http://www.mcb.org.uk/index.php?option=com_content&view=article&id=2420&Itemid=93 [accessed 22 December 2013].

Muzio, D. and Ackroyd, S. 2005. On the consequences of defensive professionalism: Recent changes in the legal labour process. *Journal of Law and Society,* 32, 615–642.

Muzio, D., Hodgson, D., Faulconbridge, J., Beaverstock, J. and Hall, S. 2011. Towards corporate professionalization: The case of project management, management consultancy and executive search. *Current Sociology,* 59, 443–464.

Muzio, D. and Kirkpatrick, I. 2011. Introduction: Professions and organizations: A conceptual framework. *Current Sociology,* 59, 389–405.

Muzio, D. and Tomlinson, J. 2012. Editorial: Researching gender, inclusion and diversity in contemporary professions and professional organizations. *Gender, Work and Organization,* 19, 455–466.

Mynatt, P., Omundson, J., Schroeder, R. and Stevens, M. 1997. The impact of Anglo and Hispanic ethnicity, gender, position, personality and job satisfaction on turnover intentions: A path analytic investigation. *Critical Perspectives on Accounting,* 8, 657–683.

Noon, M. 2007. The fatal flaws of diversity and the business case for ethnic minorities. *Work, Employment and Society,* 21, 773–784.

Noordegraaf, M. 2007. From 'pure' to 'hybrid' professionalism: Present-day professionalism in ambiguous public domains. *Administration & Society,* 39, 761–785.

North, L. 2009. Gendered experiences of industry change and the effects of neoliberalism. *Journalism Studies,* 10, 506–521.

O'Brien, R., Goetz, M., Scholte, J. and Williams, M. 2000. *Contesting Global Governance: Multilateral Economic Institutions and Global Social Movements.* Cambridge, UK: Cambridge University Press.

Office for National Statistics. 2012. *Ethnicity and National Identity in England and Wales.* London: Office for National Statistics.

Penner, A. and Saperstein, A. 2013. Engendering racial perceptions: An intersectional analysis of how social status shapes race. *Gender & Society,* 27, 319–344.

Perloff, R. M. 1993. *The Dynamics of Persuasion.* Hillsdale, NJ: Lawrence Erlbaum Associates.

Peters, T. and Waterman, R. 1982. *In Search of Excellence.* New York: HarperCollins.

Peterson, R. and Kern, R. M. 1996. From snob to omnivore. *American Sociological Review,* 61, 900–907.

Phillips, M. and Phillips, T. 1998. *Windrush: The Irresistable Rise of Multiracial Britain.* London: Harper Collins.

Philo, G., Briant, E. and Donald, P. 2013. *Bad News for Refugees.* London: Pluto Press.

Pieczka, M. 2002. Public relations expertise deconstructed. *Media, Culture and Society,* 24, 301–323.

Pieczka, M. 2007. Case studies as narrative accounts of public relations practice. *Journal of Public Relations Research,* 19, 333–356.

Pompper, D. 2004. Linking ethnic diversity and two-way symmetry: modeling female African-American practitioners' roles. *Journal of Public Relations Research,* 16, 269–299.

Pompper, D. 2005. "Difference" in public relations research: A case for introducing critical race theory. *Journal of Public Relations Research,* 17, 139–169.

Pompper, D. 2013. Interrogating inequalities perpetuated in a feminized field: Using Critical Race Theory and the intersectionality lens to render visible that which should not be disaggregated. *In:* Daymon, C. and Demetrious, K. (eds.) *Gender and Public Relations: Critical Perspectives on Voice, Image, and Identity.* London: Routledge.

PR Week. 2009. *PR Week Top 150 Consultancies 2009.* London: Haymarket.

PR Week. 2013a. *Don't Just Sit There, Do Something!* [Online]. London: Haymarket. Available at: http://www.prweek.com/article/1224686/dont-just-sit---something?DCMP= EMC-CONPRWeekly&bulletin=prweekly [accessed 23 December 2013].

PR Week. 2013b. In-house and agency heads review unpaid intern policies following campaign. *PR Week.* London: Haymarket.

PR Week/PRCA. 2011. *2011 PR Census.* London: Public Relations Consultants' Association.

Professional Associations Research Network. 2010. *Embracing E & D: What are UK professional bodies doing to embed equality and diversity into their organisations?* London: Professional Associations Research Network.

Public Relations Consultants Association. 2009. *The FrontLine Guide to a Career in PR.* London: Public Relations Consultants Association.

Public Relations Consultants Association. 2011. *What is PR?* [Online]. London: Public Relations Consultants Association [accessed 19 December 2011].

Public Relations Consultants Association. 2013a. *Diversity Network* [Online]. Available at: http://www.prca.org.uk/Diversity-Network [accessed 2 September 2013].

Public Relations Consultants Association. 2013b. *PRCA Intern Guidelines.* London: Public Relations Consultants Association.

Public Relations Consultants Association. 2013c. *PRCA Professional Charter, Public Affairs Code of Conduct, Healthcare Public Relations Code of Practice, Arbitration and Disciplinary Procedures.* London: Public Relations Consultants Association.

Puwar, N. 2004. *Space Invaders: Race, Gender and Bodies Out of Place.* Oxford, Berg.

Race for Opportunity. 2010. *Aspiration and Frustration: Ethnic Minority Hope and Reality Inside Britain's Premier Careers.* London: Business in the Community.

Ram, M. and Carter, S. 2003. Paving professional futures: Ethnic minority accountants in the United Kingdom. *International Small Business Journal,* 21, 55–71.

Ramamurthy, A. 2003. *Imperial Persuaders: Images of Africa and Asia in British Advertising,* Manchester: Manchester University Press.

Ramamurthy, A. 2012. Absences and silences: The representation of the tea picker in colonial and fair trade advertising. *Visual Culture in Britain,* 13, 367–381.

Ramdin, R. 1999. *Reimaging Britain: 500 years of Black and Asian History.* London: Pluto Press.

Richards, W. 2001. Evaluating equal opportunities initiatives: The case for a 'transformative' agenda. *In:* Noon, M. and Ogbonna, E. (eds.) *Equality, Diversity and Disadvantage in Employment.* Houndmills, Basingstoke: Palgrave.

Rollock, N. 2012. The invisibility of race: Intersectional reflections on the liminal space of alterity. *Race Ethnicity & Education,* 15, 65–84.

Said, E. 1994. *Culture and Imperialism.* London: Vintage.

Said, E. 1995. *Orientalism.* Harmondsworth: Penguin.

Schueller, M. 2009. Locating race: Global sites of postcolonial citizenship. *In:* Eze, E. (ed.) *Explorations in Postcolonial Citizenship.* Albany: State University of New York.

Sha, B. L. and Ford, R. 2007. Redefining 'requisite variety': The challenge of multiple diversities for the future of public relations excellence. *In:* Toth, E. (ed.) *Future of*

Excellence in Public Relations and Communication Management. Mahwah, NJ: Lawrence Erlbaum Associates.

Sharma, S. and Sharma, A. 2003. White paranoia: Orientalism in the age of Empire. *Fashion Theory,* 7, 301–318.

Shome, R. 2000. Outing Whiteness. *Critical Studies in Media Communication,* 17, 366–371.

Shome, R. and Hedge, R. 2002. Postcolonial approaches to communication: Charting the terrain, engaging the inheritance. *Communication Theory,* 12, 249–270.

Skeggs, B. 1994. Refusing to be civilised: 'Race', sexuality and power. *In:* Afshar, H. and Maynard, M. (eds.) *The Dynamics of Race and Gender.* London: Taylor and Francis.

Solomos, J. 2003. *Race and Racism in Britain.* Houndmills, Hants: Palgrave Macmillan.

Solomos, J. and Back, L. 1995. *Race, Politics and Social Change.* London: Routledge.

Solomos, J., Findlay, B., Jones, S. and Gilroy, P. 1982. The organic crisis of British capitalism and race: The experience of the seventies. *In:* Centre for Contemporary Cultural Studies (ed.) *The Empire Strikes Back: Race and Racism in 70s Britain.* London: Hutchinson Routledge.

Solorzano, D. G. and Yosso, T. J. 2002. Critical race methodology: Storytelling as an analytical framework for education research. *Qualitative Inquiry,* 8, 23–44.

Sommerlad, H. 2002. Women solicitors in a fractured profession: intersections of gender and professionalism in England and Wales. *International Journal of the Legal Profession,* 9, 213–234.

Sommerlad, H. 2008a. Professions, intersectionality and cultural capital: Understanding choice and constraint in occupational fields. *In*: *3rd International Legal Ethics Conference.* Queensland, Australia.

Sommerlad, H. 2008b. 'What are you doing here? You should be working in a hair salon or something'. Outsider status and professional socialization in the solicitors' profession. *Web Journal of Current Legal Issues,* 2, 1–15.

Sommerlad, H. 2009. That obscure object of desire: Sex equality and the legal profession. *In:* Hunter, R. (ed.) *Rethinking Equality Projects.* Oxford: Hart Publishing.

Sommerlad, H. and Sanderson, P. 1998. *Gender, Choice and Commitment: Women Solicitors and the Struggle for Equal Status.* Dartmouth, UK: Ashgate.

Spivak, G. C. 1988. Can the subaltern speak? *In:* Nelson, C. and Grossberg, L. (eds.) *Marxism and the Interpretation of Culture.* Urbana, IL: Univeristy of Illlinois Press.

Sriramesh, K. 2002. The dire need for multiculturalism in public relations education: An Asian perspective. *Journal of Communication Management,* 7, 54–70.

Sriramesh, K. and Verčič, D. 2009. *The Global Public Relations Handbook: Theory, Research and Practice.* New York: Routledge.

Steinbugler, A., Press, J. and Dias, J. 2006. Gender, race, and affirmative action – operationalizing intersectionality in survey research. *Gender & Society,* 20, 805–825.

Sue, D. W., Capodilupo, C. M., Torino, G. C., Bucceri, J. M., Holder, A. M. B., Nadal, K. L. et al. 2007. Racial microaggressions in everyday life: Implications for clinical practice. *American Psychologist,* 62, 271–286.

Surma, A. and Daymon, C. 2013. Caring about public relations and the gendered cultural intermediary role. *In:* Daymon, C. and Demetrious, K. (eds.) *Gender and Public Relations: Critical Perspectives on Voice, Image, and Identity.* Abingdon, Oxon: Routledge.

Syvedain, H. 1993. Major Minority Interest. *Marketing.* London: Haymarket Publications.

Tallents, S. 1932. *The Projection of England.* London: Olen Press.

The Law Society. 2009. *Response to the call for evidence on Fair Access to the Professions: A submission on the solicitors' profession by the Law Society.* London: The Law Society.

The Panel on Fair Access to the Professions. 2009. *Unleashing aspiration: The final report of the Panel on Fair Access to the Professions*. London: Cabinet Office.

Thornton, M. 1996. *Dissonance and Distrust: Women in the Legal Profession*. Melbourne: Oxford University Press.

Tindall, N. 2007. *Identity, power, and difference: The management of roles and self among public relations practitioners*. University of Maryland, College Park.

Tindall, N. 2009. In search of career satisfaction: African-American public relations practitioners, pigeonholing, and the workplace. *Public Relations Review*, 35, 443–445.

Tindall, N. T. and Waters, R. D. 2012. Coming out to tell our stories: Using Queer Theory to understand the career experiences of gay men in public relations. *Journal of Public Relations Research*, 24, 451–475.

Toledano, M. 2010. Professional competition and cooperation in the digital age: A pilot study of New Zealand practitioners. *Public Relations Review*, 36, 230–237.

Toth, E. and Cline, C. 2007. Women in public relations: Success linked to organizational and societal cultures. *In:* Creedon, P. and Cramer, J. (eds.) *Women in Mass Communication*, 3rd ed. Thousand Oaks, CA: Sage.

Trethewey, A. 1997. Resistance, identity, and empowerment: A postmodern feminist analysis of clients in a human service organization. *Communication Monographs*, 64, 281–301.

Tyrell, N. 1998. Ethnic PR comes off the sidelines. *PRWeek*. London: Haymarket.

Valentine, G. 2007. Theorizing and researching intersectionality: A challenge for feminist geography. *The Professional Geographer*, 59, 10–21.

Vardeman-Winter, J. 2011. Confronting Whiteness in public relations campaigns and research with women. *Journal of Public Relations Research*, 23, 412–441.

Vardeman-Winter, J. and Tindall, N. 2010. 'If it's a woman's issue, I pay attention to it': Gendered and intersectional complications in The Heart Truth media campaign [Online]. *PRism*, 7. Available at: http://www.prismjournal.org/fileadmin/Praxis/Files/Gender/VardemanWinter_Tindall.pdf

Walby, S. 2007. Complexity theory, systems theory and multiple intersecting social inequalities. *Philosophy of the Social Sciences*, 22, 449–470.

Warde, A. and Gayo-Cal, M. 2009. The anatomy of cultural omnivorousness: The case of the United Kingdom. *Poetics*, 37, 119–145.

Watson, T. and Noble, G. 2007. *Evaluating Public Relations: A Best Practice Guide to Public Relations Research, Planning and Evaluation*. London: Kogan Page.

Waymer, D. (ed.) 2012. *Culture, Social Class and Race in Public Relations: Perspectives and Applications*. Plymouth: Lexington Books.

Webb, J. 1997. The politics of equal opportunity. *Gender, Work & Organization*, 4, 159–169.

Weber Shandwick. 2007. *The Multi-Cultural Insight study: Understanding the Multicultural Market*. London: Weber Shandwick.

Weisenfeld, L. and Robinson-Backmon, I. 2007. Upward mobility and the African American accountant: An analysis of perceived discrimination, perceived career advancement curtailment, and intent to remain. *Accounting and the Public Interest*, 7, 26–49.

Wellington, C. and Bryson, J. 2001. At face value? Image consultancy, emotional labour and professional work. *Sociology*, 35, 933–946.

Werbner, P. 2013. Everyday multiculturalism: Theorising the difference between 'intersectionality' and 'multiple identities'. *Ethnicities*, 13, 401–419.

Wernick, A. 1991. *Promotional Culture: Advertising, Ideology and Symbolic Expression*. London, Sage.

Windahl, S. and Signitzer, B. 1992. *Using Communication Theory.* London: Sage.

Winker, G. and Degele, N. 2011. Intersectionality as multi-level analysis: Dealing with social inequality. *European Journal of Women's Studies,* 18, 51–66.

Witz, A. 1992. *Professions and Patriarchy.* London: Routledge.

Wyatt, R. 2013. The PR census 2013. *PRWeek.* London: Haymarket.

Yaxley, H. 2013. Career experiences of women in British public relations (1970–1989). *Public Relations Review,* 39, 156–165.

Yeomans, L. 2013. Gendered performance and identity in PR consulting relationships: A UK perspective. *In:* Daymon, C. and Demetrious, K. (eds.) *Gender and Public Relations: Critical Perspectives on Voice, Image, and Identity.* Abingdon, Oxon: Routledge.

Yosso, T. J. 2005. Whose culture has capital? A critical race theory discussion of community cultural wealth. *Race, Ethnicity and Education,* 8, 69–91.

Yuval-Davis, N. 2006. Intersectionality and feminist politics. *European Journal of Women's Studies,* 13, 193–209.

Yuval-Davis, N., Anthias, F. and Kofman, E. 2005. Secure borders and safe haven and the gendered politics of belonging: Beyond social cohesion. *Ethnic and Racial Studies,* 28, 513–535.

Zanoni, P. and Janssens, M. 2004. Deconstructing difference: The rhetoric of human resource managers' diversity discourses. *Organization Studies,* 24, 55–74.

Zanoni, P. and Janssens, M. 2007. Minority employees engaging with (diversity) management: An analysis of control, agency and micro-emancipation. *Journal of Management Studies,* 1–27.

Zerbinos, E. and Clanton, G. A. 1993. Minority practitioners: Career influences, job satisfaction, and discrimination. *Public Relations Review,* 19, 75–91.

Zinn, M. and Thornton Dill, B. 1996. Theorizing difference from multiracial feminism. *Feminist Studies,* 22, 321–331.

Index

Note: page number in **bold** refer to a table, figures, or box.